CUSTOMER FOCUS - THE SID™ WAY

A Self-Initiated Development Workbook for Leaders and Managers

Ben McDonald

Sidney McDonald

BENCHMARK
Learning International

CUSTOMER FOCUS – THE SID™ WAY
A Self-Initiated Development Workbook for Leaders and Managers

Benchmark Learning International
5239 Quarterpath Drive
Boise, ID 83716 U.S.A.

http://www.thesidway.com

ISBN-13: 978-061544080-4

ISBN-10: 061544080-0

Large quantity purchase of this book is available at a discount from the publisher. For more information, contact the sales department at BenchMark Learning International, Inc. 1-208-433-9093 or write to Sales Director, BenchMark Learning International, 5239 Quarterpath Drive, Boise, ID 83716 U.S.A.

To the Future Leaders

Sean
Heather
Coreena
Luke
Caleb
Lydia

Table of Contents

Preface

When this workbook was in its infancy and research stage, our economy was booming and the markets were soaring. Finding talent for open positions was difficult because the best people were working and being promoted. However, the principles that drive booming economic times have changed, thus leaving those individuals who have taken passive and shortcut approaches to professional development and business in general at a disadvantage.

Even if you were one who was charging full-speed ahead with your own leadership development, current times call for even more focused use of proven measures to stay successful. Now more than ever you must work hard to develop the skills and behaviors to get ahead and thrive as a leader. It has always been *your* responsibility; now more than ever it is up to *you.*

Some of the consequences of tough economic times are seen in organizations struggling to find ways to keep people employed. This is usually achieved by cutting costs as much as possible, and often the first programs to go are employee and leadership development. Our self-initiated development workbook series fills the gap that is created and positions the individual and organization for long-term success.

The best way to thrive as a leader and have sustainable professional and business results is to self initiate your own personal leadership development in a thoughtful and systematic approach. This approach is not only valuable for you to improve your effectiveness and to see an increase in your results, but also benefits your organization. If your organization is successful, your position is more secure.

As professional coaches we have seen leaders that have engaged, worked hard, changed needed behaviors and adopted new skills. The results were noticed by others and consequently they were able to advance into new and more rewarding positions. On the other hand, we have also seen leaders who have been complacent in their professional development. Eventually they lose credibility in their position and their results suffer.

We have always believed that development and improvement are the responsibility of the individual, even when leadership development opportunities are available, and that an individual can go as far as they want in their career if they have the motivation, tools and skills. Even if you have the most expensive and renowned leadership coach or training program at your disposal, it will do you no good if you do not personally engage. This workbook and the others in our series are the result of that belief and provide you with:

- Vital leadership principles that will fine tune your leadership skills and behaviors
- Processes to follow to achieve success
- Methods to identify your most pressing leadership needs
- Tools and resources to increase your effectiveness

Following our process may not always be easy. It requires honest self assessment, time and disciplined work on your part; however, the rewards will be worth it. We ask that you take a candid look at yourself and then take action based on what you see. Success is up to you. We cannot guarantee success; however, we can guarantee that if you complete this workbook you will know more about yourself and what you need to do to improve and become more effective as a leader, especially in customer focus. We will be your guide and provide the step-by-step coaching as you walk through our self-initiated development model; the effort and results are in your hands.

We Wrote This Workbook For You!

If you are currently in or aspiring to a leadership or management position, if you have the desire to be successful and make a positive impact in your sphere of influence, this book is for you. If you are in a threatened industry or any organization that is undergoing "belt tightening;" self-initiated development is especially important because you need to differentiate yourself from competition. If you have lost your position in leadership or management, what better time than now to methodically work to improve your skills and behaviors in preparation for a future position. Finally, if you are successful in your current position and see yourself retiring within the next ten years, this book is vital for you too because during the last years of your career it is easy to think you do not need to improve your customer-focused skills and can risk becoming complacent.

Your Coaching Team

As your coaches throughout this workbook, we will impart not only our knowledge of customer-focused skills and behaviors, but also many of the lessons we have learned from our clients. We, like most others at the onset of a career, began near the bottom of an organization and worked hard while actively engaging in a variety of continuous learning activities. Our careers have taken us through the doors of various industries and organizations, and prior to our own leadership development and coaching practice, included operations, sales, and human resources experiences. Within each of these positions and experiences our leadership responsibilities increased, eventually taking us into senior leadership positions.

During the leadership development phase of our careers we began working more closely with leaders in identifying those skills and behaviors that promote effectiveness, results and advancement. Along with extensive research over the past 20 years, we have refined the competencies that successful leaders exemplify and the tools used to promote results within these core competencies. This research and experience are the basis for our leadership competency model which is shown in Appendix D in Part 3 of this book and is the basis of our self-initiated development series of 30 workbooks addressing the most important competencies for leadership and management positions.

Final Thoughts Before You Begin

Make the time for yourself to achieve your dreams and success, starting with developing your skills in customer focus. Constantly think of the benefits you will receive from developing your leadership skills. YOU are the one responsible for this gaining these benefits. Your future is waiting and there is no better time to start the path toward achieving your goals than now.

Acknowledgments

This book would not be a reality without the unwavering support of many individuals. First, we wish to thank our many clients from whom we have learned so much. It is in their organizations that we have been able to form, test, and improve upon the concepts used in this book. We do not have the space to name each client and individual but we will personally thank them.

To the hundreds of leaders and managers that we have coached and advised, we thank you for your openness to our style and our pushing you to be your best. We recognize that it is not easy to be coached, but have seen the positive results and achievements you have made.

Our mentors in the past have contributed through pointing out our own self-initiated development paths we have followed. We owe much to Dominic Costa, Frank McSparren, President John Anderson of Illinois Institute of Technology, Nancy Atwood, Bill Doherty, and Linda Simmons. We have learned from your successes and respect you all as leaders.

Others have contributed to our efforts by reviewing our draft manuscripts or brainstorming ideas with us. A special thanks to Kalvin and Liz Evans for their valuable reviews and feedback. Liz is a creative genius. Vicki Morningstar, Bob Bynum, and Kevin Bell also added their touch and wealth of experience in leadership, especially self-initiated leadership development.

Four people that have inspired us over the years to be our best: Bob McDonald was a farmer who only had an 8th grade education. Nevertheless, he knew more about integrity, trust, and common sense than most CEO's. Carlean Huntington inspired us to always be courageous, to believe in ourselves, and to contribute to the success of others. Lee and Connie Bevins continue to believe in us and provide loving support when most needed.

As "students of leadership" we have also been influenced by other successful leaders, some of whom we know and others that we simply observe because they are the best at what they do. These include Pastor Paul Hatfield of The Pursuit church in Boise, Idaho, Coach Chris Petersen of Boise State University, John Maxwell, General Ron Fogleman (USAF retired), and Carrie Pelzel of Dartmouth College.

"Destiny is not a matter of chance; it is a matter of choice. It is not a thing to be waited for; it is a thing to be achieved."
-William Jennings Bryan

"Sam Walton's values are: treat the customer right, take care of your people, be honest in your dealings, pass savings along to the customer, keep things simple, think small, control costs and continuously improve operations."
- Michael Bergdahl

Coaches' Questions to Ponder

Why do you want to develop your customer-focused skills and behaviors?

What attempts have you made in the past to develop your leadership skills and behaviors? Have they been successful? What could you have done differently?

Do you believe that professional development is your responsibility or the responsibility of your organization?

Introduction

Welcome to *Customer Focus — The SID Way; A Self-Initiated Development Workbook for Leaders and Managers*. Self-Initiated Development (SID™) is the future of learning and the path toward achieving your professional goals. Our purpose in developing our SID™ series for leaders and managers is to provide a tool to identify strengths and weaknesses in your professional skills and behaviors and provide a model for you to take charge of your own development.

The following FAQs will help you better understand SID™ and the role of this customer-focused workbook.

Who Should Use Self-Initiated Development?

SID™ is designed for you to take charge of your own professional development and can be used alone or in conjunction with other development tools; so the simple answer to who should use self-initiated development is — anyone who wants to improve their professional skills and achieve their goals. Many people may say, "But I have a degree." Or "My company provides training for me to improve." In response to these questions, anyone with at least a day of experience in a company or organization knows there is much more to learn than what they received from their degree program. What they have learned may be valuable, but there is so much more to learn about application and skills and behaviors that higher education cannot address.

Additionally, most experienced professionals realize that while their company may provide some training, they are not typically capable of handling all leadership development activities and in today's economic climate, fewer and fewer companies and organizations are providing sufficient leadership and management training programs. It is a simple economic fact that when times are lean, professional development is one of the first areas to be cut. We believe that whether professional development is provided by your organization or not, YOU are the one responsible for improving and achieving your goals. SID™ will help you do that and clearly differentiate you from others.

How Does This Workbook Fit Into the Overall SID™ Program?

SID™ is a proven development process; this workbook is a tool to help you achieve better customer focus as part of that process. We have developed over thirty workbooks to supplement the SID™ process for leaders. You can select which workbooks to use based on your self assessment across each of the 30 leadership competencies. More about the SID™ process will come later. We will also give you extensive guidance on how to use this workbook to achieve the maximum benefit on your route to achieving your customer focus goals.

How Did We Select the 30 Leadership Competencies?

We have a combined 40 years experience in leadership development, working with corporate, non-profit, and university organizations. Our selection of the most relevant competencies comes from our experience in giving online leadership assessments, presenting workshops, and facilitating retreats for leadership teams around the world. In addition, we have reviewed most of the "literature" and models that have been published over the past 20 years. We are confident that our broad look at the competencies that make up leadership skills and behaviors is the best approach to take to provide readers with targeted goals to improve their leadership skills.

4P's Competency Model™

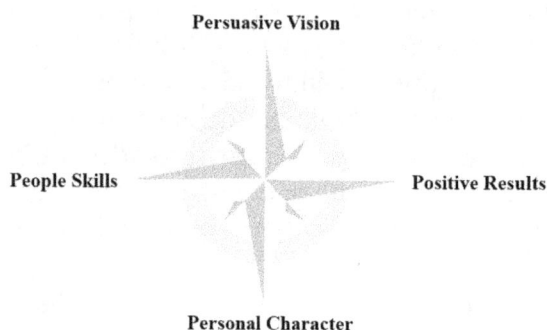

Persuasive Vision

People Skills

Positive Results

Personal Character

Our 30 competencies are organized using our 4P's Competency Model™ which is represented by a compass. The competencies are divided between each of the four compass heading titles. Customer Focus is in the Positive Results compass heading.

You can see which "P" each competency falls under in Appendix D. We encourage you to review this list and order the workbooks most appropriate to your position and professional goals.

You can also contact us at questions@thesidway.com to receive our master self assessment. By completing this master self assessment, you can determine which competencies are your strengths and which are the areas you should most focus on improving.

How is this Workbook Organized?

There are three distinct parts to the workbook. First, you will be given an overview of our Self-Initiated Development (SID™) Model and be introduced to how it can help you identify, assess, and improve in the competencies needed for your current and/or future position.

The second part to the workbook provides the content, exercises, and case studies that are at the heart of your efforts to improve your customer-focused skills and behaviors. You should spend most of your time with this section of the workbook.

The final part to the workbook, including the appendices, provides the tools needed to complete a development plan to achieve your goals. The appendices include tools you can use in the future and the "Coaches' Bookshelf" provides additional reading resources.

In summary, the workbook is organized as follows:

- Part 1 – The SID™ Model
- Part 2 – Customer Focus Content and Workbook
- Part 3 – Development Resources and Appendices, including the Coaches' Itinerary with specific customer focus developmental recommendations

What is Our Coaching Approach to Developing Leaders in this Workbook?

The content in this book is designed for you to learn more about customer focus yourself. However, our role is to be your "Coach." We are leadership coaches and have found in our work that self-initiated development may not be the only choice you have to improve your skills, but it may be the best method for you to learn.

As your coaches, we recommend that you read the content and do all the exercises in the order provided. The "How to Use the Customer Focus Workbook" section provides you with valuable suggestions on how to use this book, particularly Parts 2 and 3. If you have any questions, feel free to e-mail your question to questions@thesidway.com. One of your coaches will get back to you within 24 hours with a response.

Note From Your Coaches

As mentioned, this workbook is in three parts. If you are ready to give your attention to improving your customer-focused skills and behaviors, go directly to Part 2. However, if you want to learn more about our Self-Initiated Development Model that we use in coaching and is the foundation for how we guide you to develop using this workbook, begin with Part 1.

"I am still learning."

\- Michelangelo

"Why don't they pass a constitutional amendment prohibiting anybody from learning anything? If it works as well as prohibition did, in five years Americans would be the smartest race of people on Earth."

\- Will Rogers

Coaches' Questions to Ponder

Who has helped you in your personal development? Who has helped you in your professional development? How did they do this? Were you receptive?

Part 1 – The Self-Initiated Development (SID™) Model

"Life is a classroom. Only those who are willing to be lifelong learners will move to the head of the class."

- Zig Ziglar

As you will learn in a moment, professional development is an ongoing process and its initiation and completion is up to YOU. You can become a better leader if YOU desire; you will have difficulty if you lack the initiative or the desire.

Our SID™ Model stresses the importance of taking responsibility for your own development and provides a framework for your development efforts. Following this straight-forward development process, that you are in charge of and accountable to, you will have a path to increase your effectiveness as a leader or manager.

Self-Initiated Development Background

Self-initiated development is a principle that is at the very fabric of our world from its inception and is a critical component for personal and professional success. For centuries, people have had to be self-reliant in many areas of life to succeed, and in some cases to even survive. There are countless examples of people in history and in the present day that have had a vision, determined a path to achieve their vision, and have done the work necessary to succeed; sometimes at much effort, trial and error, and sacrifice. Although working with others toward achieving common goals is also a critical factor to achieving success, without individual motivation and drive along a pre-determined path, our outcomes can be severely thwarted and stalled.

From the beginning, others help in our development. When we are small children our parents help us with everything, even eating and learning how to go to the toilet. As we become older we still get help developing through teachers, family, and coaches. Others help us develop in a myriad of ways – physically, emotionally, and intellectually; and for some spiritually. Even in college we develop with the help of our professors and teaching assistants. Then we get to our first "real" job. Many organizations have programs for entry-level employees, but often we develop through on-the-job training. Then, as we gain experience and combine it with the right attitudes and skills, we are promoted to more challenging positions and we continue to refine our skills and influence through further development.

Self-initiated and directed development is a powerful force as Carl Rogers, an eminent psychologist asserted, "Anything that can be taught to another is relatively inconsequential, and has little or no significant influence on behavior." Likewise, he adds, "The only learning which significantly influences behavior is self-discovered self-appropriated learning."

A valid example of the power self-initiated development can be seen in Abraham Lincoln's life. He confirms the concept of self-initiated development and success when he said to "bear in mind, your own resolution to succeed is more important than any other one thing." He goes further to say of himself that, "I'll study and prepare, and when the time comes I'll be ready." This philosophy and drive were part of the reason for his great success despite a marginal formal education.

Development is a life-long process and involves many facets of learning. For success to be achieved during this process we have to be self-disciplined, motivated, and aware of our ultimate goal. For that reason, we have created a self-initiated development process that through years of research and working with leaders has proven to help people achieve their success and advance in their profession.

Self-Initiated vs. Organizational-Initiated Development

In many ways, our changing culture has given us messages that are not always conducive to self-initiated development. We have become reliant on others to tell us what we should do and set the path for us; in essence our reliance has shifted from ourselves to others, often unintentionally, in the organization we are associated. As previously mentioned, it is important to have others involved in achieving great outcomes; however, the subtle message we often get is that "we" will do it for you, just follow "our" plan.

One example of this can be found in the organizational setting by well meaning organizations bringing employee and leadership development to new levels in order to raise the talent of their workforce. Rightfully so, this has been and still is a necessary component in an ever-changing and competitive landscape. However, the dilemma is that over the years employees have often become reliant on their employer for professional development and the path toward professional success; consequently, in many cases individual motivation for growth dwindles as it becomes a "have to" training and development event rather than a personal "passion" to grow and achieve greater things for self and organization.

In addition, today's economy is driving many organizations to eliminate costly training and development programs. However, this does not eliminate an individual's need to continually improve their skills and behaviors to become a better leader. That is why sustainable development must now focus on "self initiation."

Self-initiated development is not meant to replace organizational development initiatives and is not meant to promote a "lone ranger" mentality that abandons the importance of teamwork endeavors; after all, in business and in life we need others and those we work with are important in our career success and many times to our professional advancement. When looking at an organization's development initiatives it is wise for us to remember that the organization cannot provide all things for our development. Organizational development programs are often at the mercy of the organization's leaders, its ability to fund these initiatives, and are confined to the culture within which they are constructed. Therefore, this gives us even more reason to take our professional development and success into our own hands because ultimately we are in control and can shape the outcome and keep it sustainable.

Who Should Initiate Self Development?

So how do we weave the concept of self-initiated development into our current situation so that we may advance from where we are now and set ourselves on a path that leads us to reach our professional goals? The first important key to remember is that it is about *your* development, *your* passions, *your* goals, and *your* success. The bottom line is that you are a unique individual with goals, dreams, and aspirations as well as talents, strengths, and certainly a few weaknesses. You know where you want to go in your professional life (together with or separate from your current employer), what interests you, and may even have an idea of the path toward goal achievement. The model to follow for self-initiated development is meant to support you in achieving your goals through a systematic process in which you are in control; therefore, you control the outcome (and success) as well. You have full responsibility for the process and can take it as far as you need or desire.

So who should initiate and direct their own professional development? The answer is everyone! Young, old, successful, self-employed, unemployed, students, leaders of organizations and anyone else aspiring to be successful or advance their career should be on a systematic process for self development. It is important to remember that no one is going to do it for you although you may have guides along the way to provide assistance. If your job title or function is like any of the following, this book is for you:

- Executives and other senior leaders (C-level, V.P. level, Director level)
- General manager
- Project manager
- Sales manager
- Technical manager
- Training manager
- Team leader
- Entrepreneur and small business owner
- Business development manager
- Anyone aspiring to the above positions

Different organizations (corporations, higher education, government, non-profit, entrepreneur) may have different titles, but you get the picture. Anyone who is in a leadership or management position (or those who aspire to these positions) will benefit from this book.

One of the goals of this book is to challenge your paradigms around how to achieve professional growth and advancement as well as provide a framework and the supporting tools in which you can be personally responsible for realizing your professional success. Most important, we hope to encourage the growth of our current and future leaders; for with you at your best, our businesses, schools and non-profit organizations will be more successful and your impact can and will make a positive difference in our world.

Self-Initiated Development vs. Self Improvement

Some may point out that there are hundreds, if not thousands, of books and articles on how to improve. Primarily, these resources focus on your self improvement. Although we advocate self improvement to develop yourself as a well-balanced person, our focus is on the specific skills and behaviors needed in your professional life. Few books or articles exist that clearly give the professional effective steps to own their professional development and succeed at achieving professional goals.

Examples may be in order to clarify the differences between self-initiated development and self improvement. First, an example of self-initiated development:

Lily knew after a few years that Caso, Inc. was the company for her. She loved the challenges and the opportunities available to her. But, she knew that she needed to improve her professional skills to achieve her goal of becoming Vice President of Operations. Her first step was to identify, through an assessment, what her strong and weak areas were in leadership and management. The assessment, coupled with the requirements for her desired position, helped her realize that her strengths included communication skills, time management, and integrity. Her weaknesses, relevant to the position, included strategic thinking, teamwork, and financial management. Then, using the results as a guide, she put together her objectives and the steps to improve in her weak areas and capitalize on her strengths. Her assessment provided her with concrete ideas on what her development steps should be and their priority.

Although it was a lot of work, it paid off for Lily. She became Vice President of Operations within three years.

Self improvement is somewhat different, as this example illustrates:

Dale was happy at Kentron Industries. His job gave him plenty of time to enjoy his family and his hobbies. He had a problem with time management, however. He never seemed to be able to get to work on time and he missed a lot of deadlines. His manager talked to him frequently about this and encouraged him to "fix the problem" or face some consequences. Dale was a little resistant because he felt he worked hard, but he agreed to look at ways to improve. He bought a book on time management and implemented some of the ideas. Over time, he became better at meeting deadlines and managed to get to work on time on a regular basis.

Dale's change pleased his boss and even he was happier because there seemed to be less stress on him. He settled into a new routine and was even able to focus more on his family and hobbies.

What are the differences between these two situations? First, Lily had a long-term goal that *she* set after considering her future in detail. In Dale's case, his improvement was necessitated because of poor performance, and facing negative consequences he reluctantly took steps to improve. Lily developed objectives and took steps to get an objective assessment of her strengths and weaknesses. Dale simply bought a book to get hints on doing better in one particular area. Lily achieved her goal through using a myriad of developmental resources to progress methodically along her long-term path. Dale became complacent again once he overcame one weakness.

Self-initiated development is an active process leading toward a professional goal. It is positive. Self improvement, although the outcome may be positive in some ways, focuses on correcting (often due to the demands of others) a negative attribute.

The SID™ Model

As coaches, we have developed a holistic approach to leadership development using the SID™ Model (shown on the next page) to enable individuals to increase their effectiveness. The model, although simple and straightforward, does require one key ingredient on behalf of the participant – motivation. The SID™ Model provides the guidelines and framework; you provide the motivation and self discipline to succeed. On the following pages, after the model, we explain more about each step.

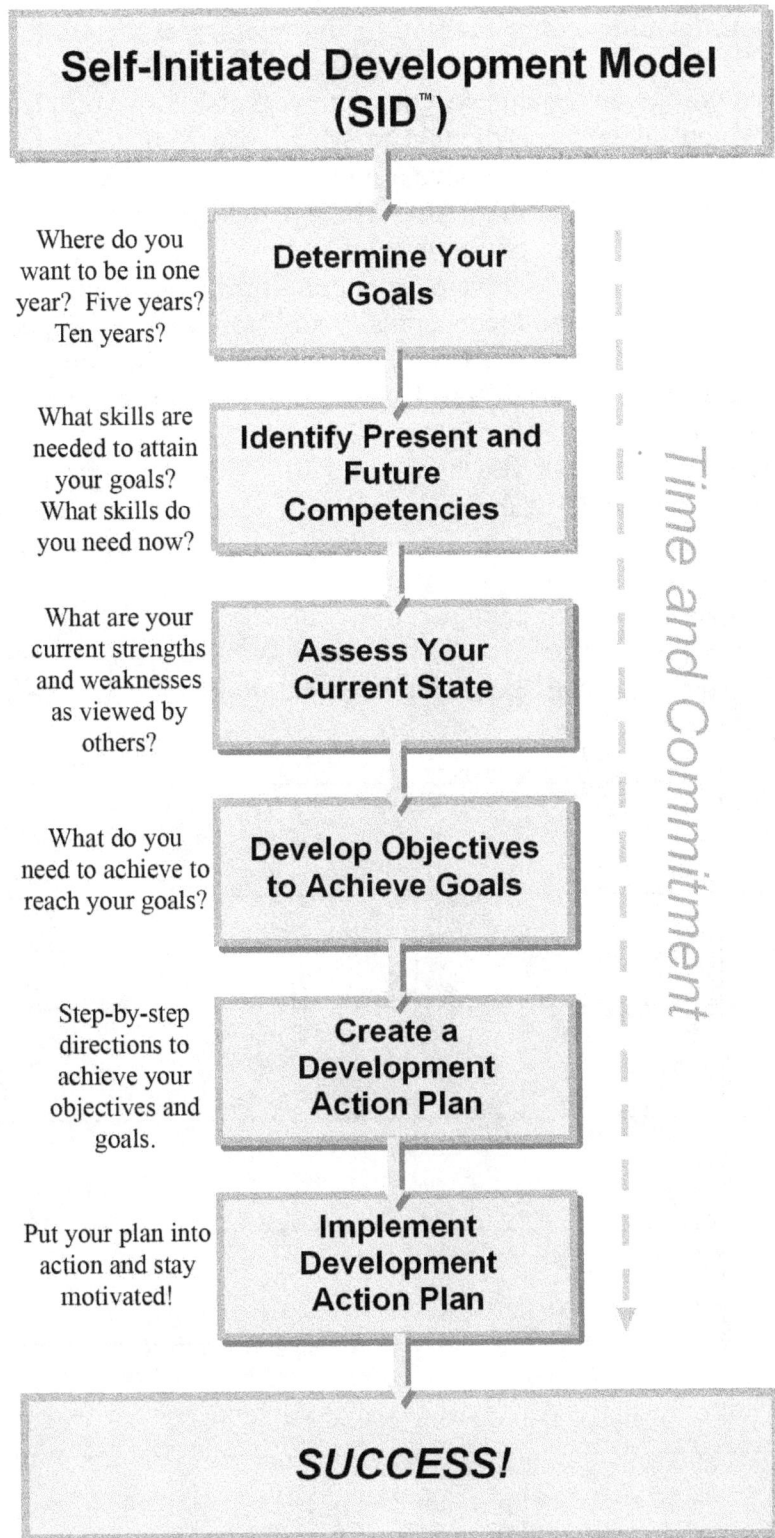

Self-Initiated Development Model (SID™)

Where do you want to be in one year? Five years? Ten years?	**Determine Your Goals**	
What skills are needed to attain your goals? What skills do you need now?	**Identify Present and Future Competencies**	*Time and Commitment*
What are your current strengths and weaknesses as viewed by others?	**Assess Your Current State**	
What do you need to achieve to reach your goals?	**Develop Objectives to Achieve Goals**	
Step-by-step directions to achieve your objectives and goals.	**Create a Development Action Plan**	
Put your plan into action and stay motivated!	**Implement Development Action Plan**	

SUCCESS!

Step One – Determine Your Goals

Have you given thought to your future goals? Can you clearly articulate them? Have you given much thought to where you want to be in a year? Five years? Ten years? Many people have a muddled sense of where they want to be, but are not clear about either their goals or the path to get there.

We recommend that you give a lot of thought during the initial phase of self-initiated development to your personal and professional goals for the future. Goals should be realistic, both conceptually and from a time perspective. It is not realistic to set a goal to become the CEO of a Fortune 500 company in the next year if you are currently a mid-level manager in a small company. Be realistic when setting your goals.

Explore what makes you happy and fills your day with joy and energy. Perhaps your goals should be more aligned with your happiness than the financial compensation.

Personal Reflection

Using the following chart, list your future goals for 1 year, 2 years, 5 years, and 10 years.

	GOAL
1 YEAR	
1 YEAR	
1 YEAR	
1 YEAR	
2 YEARS	

2 YEARS	
2 YEARS	
2 YEARS	
5 YEARS	
5 YEARS	
5 YEARS	
10 YEARS	
10 YEARS	
10 YEARS	

After thinking about your goals; write a paragraph about each. Then, list the benefits of achieving each goal. The better you can articulate a goal and its benefits, the easier it is going to be to take the steps to achieve it and maintain your motivation.

Step Two – Identify Present and Future Competencies

A competency is a skill, attitude, or behavior that is required to do a particular job. Although a job may require some technical competencies, we are currently concerned with those that are management or leadership oriented. Entry-level competencies may include problem solving, communications, teamwork and integrity. More senior level positions may include competencies such as strategic thinking, motivation, conflict management, and influencing. Competencies are position specific and often identified in a person's job description.

For self-initiated development we encourage participants to not only identify and assess their performance on competencies for their current position but also the position they may aspire to attain. This gives a more thorough perspective in preparing for the future.

Competencies are measured using assessment items. A group of items measure each competency. For example, an item that measures communication skills may be: *Develops excellent customer presentations.* Other communication items would be included in the assessment that would measure other aspects of communication skills, such as written communications, oral communications, and client/customer communication skills.

By identifying your present and future competency needs you can have a clear understanding of what is required for you to be effective and successful in your current and desired positions. Remember, these competencies are those skills and behaviors you need to do well to be successful in your current or desired position.

Personal Reflection

Review the following list of competencies. Check which apply to your current position and which apply to a position to which you aspire.

COMPETENCY	APPLIES TO CURRENT POSITION (√)	APPLIES TO DESIRED POSITION (√)
Business Development		
Change Leadership		
Commitment to Diversity		
Commitment to Quality		
Communication		
Conflict Management		
Courage		
Creativity		
Credibility		
Customer Focus		
Decision Making		
Financial Management		
Focus on Results		
Followership		
Influencing		
Initiative		
Inspiration		
Integrity		
Interpersonal Skills		
Motivation		
Negotiation		
Planning		
Problem Solving		
Strategic Thinking		
Stress Management		
Talent Management		
Teamwork		
Technical Skills		
Time Management		
Trust		

These competencies are covered in the BenchMark Learning International workbook series. We recommend that you complete the master self assessment on our website (http://www.thesidway.com) to determine your strengths and which areas you should focus on improving. The remainder of this book provides the content and exercises to improve your customer-focused skills and behaviors.

Step 3 – Assess Your Current State

The third step of the SID™ Model is to assess your current state for each competency either through a self assessment or a 360° assessment that gets feedback from a larger group of people. The "Know Your Heading" section in Part 2 of this book includes a self assessment for Customer Focus. The difficulty with a self assessment is that you must be totally honest and transparent with yourself. The results may be quite different from a 360° assessment that takes into account the perceptions of others.

However, the self assessment is an excellent way to start identifying your strengths and weaknesses. Based on the results of your self assessment you can then move to the next step.

Step 4 – Develop Objectives to Achieve Goals

After reviewing the results of your self assessment and you have determined the competencies you want to focus on, next develop a set of objectives to improve your skills and behaviors in these areas. Objectives may be designed to enhance a person's strengths or, more often, to overcome identified weaknesses.

Objectives should be SMART – Specific, Measurable, Attainable, Relevant, and Timely. Let's look at SMART objectives in more detail.

Specific – Objectives need to be specific. For example, *I will improve my customer focus*, is not specific. What part of customer focus is your weakness? A more specific objective would be: *I will read the developmental recommendations regarding how to communicate more effectively with customers by March 30.*

Measurable – Objectives should be measurable so that you know when they are attained or how much progress is being made. Using our previous example, a measurable objective would be: *I will read the 4 development recommendations regarding how to communicate more effectively with customers by March 30.* This is measurable; you know how much you have accomplished and how much is remaining to do.

Attainable – Although we have already established that self-initiated development is a lot of work and requires discipline, you must be realistic with what you can accomplish. Try not to focus on too much in too limited time. This will only serve to frustrate you. Stress results, not quantity.

Relevant – Following the general development recommendations provided with each competency will keep your objectives relevant. Sometimes, however, we may pursue an avenue that is not relevant to what we want to achieve. Be careful and stay focused on what is important to achieve.

Timely – Schedule is important! Evaluate everything you need to do as part of your development plan and realistically schedule the actions you need to take to achieve each objective. In our above example, you would schedule the reading of each of the development recommendations and the date you schedule the last to be finished is the date you will achieve that objective.

As mentioned, objectives are supported by the actions necessary to achieve them. When all the actions are accomplished the objective is achieved. The next step is to create the actions to achieve the objectives.

Step 5 – Create a Development Action Plan

The most important part of preparing to improve is the developmental action plan. Without it your efforts may not be focused and even though you have specific objectives to achieve your goals you may not be successful without a plan. Later in this workbook we will help you create a developmental action plan based on the results of your self assessment.

Step 6 – Implementing Your Development Action Plan

Now the hard part begins. The self assessment process is over and you have created your development action plan based on your self assessment scores. If you follow the plan, you will achieve each objective and ultimately your goal. The biggest problems that people encounter when implementing their action plan are that they allow obstacles to steal their time away from the direction of the plan. Or, they are easily distracted because they do not see immediate results. Here are some tips to successfully implement your action plan.

- Set a date to start your development steps for each competency. Mark it on your calendar and make it an important day.

- List your goals and put them in a very visible place so that you see them every day.

- Next to each goal, list the benefits of achieving it. Review the benefits daily.

- When you complete an action step (reading an article or book, completing an exercise) mark it off in your plan.

- Don't get discouraged if you get off schedule. Life happens and we are not always able to stay on schedule. Review your schedule and determine how you can make up time.

- Review the results of your self assessment periodically to reinforce to yourself that you are on the right track.

- Celebrate successes. If you are taking steps to improve your decision making, celebrate when you change behaviors in this area, especially when you see the positive results!

- Share your plan with a family member or trusted colleague. Ask them to be an accountability partner. Meet with them regularly to show your results.

- Don't be afraid to tweak your goals or objectives if you change your direction slightly. New opportunities are always entering our lives and you need to be adaptable.

Final Considerations

Another reason for implementing self-initiated development is competition. In today's world, we face fierce competition and it increases everyday. Competition does not just happen at the organizational level, but also at the individual level and having the ability to positively differentiate yourself in the "crowd" will only increase your likelihood of reaching your goals (or, in today's environment, maintaining your employment).

When you look at today's world with unknown economic times ahead, we should all be prepared to differentiate ourselves because those that are viewed as self-starters, motivated, and as having the greatest overall skills and behaviors are the ones that will land the jobs, get the promotions, succeed in their current position, succeed in their small businesses, and be able to influence others with integrity to attain success.

Finally, those that initiate and direct their own professional development reap the rewards of success. This certainly may be monetary, but you will also find that these people are usually those that are happy, the highest earners, and highly respected by others.

Part 2 – Customer Focus

Introduction

What is a business without customers? Simple – out of business. All organizations have customers and they provide the revenue to keep the organization alive and growing. Think of a business or organization that does not have customers. You can't. Therefore, it is important that everyone pay attention to and focus on their customers.

Most of us also have internal customers – those to whom we are accountable for inputs or use our goods or services within the organization. Some parts of a business or organization only have internal customers. Too often we forget that the relationship between someone in facilities management and a project manager, for example, is a supplier – customer relationship.

Objectives

This workbook, from the BenchMark Learning International Self-Initiated Development for Leaders and Managers Series, is designed to help you improve your customer-focused skills and behaviors. After reading this book and completing the exercises you will be able to:

- State the importance of customer focus for a leader and the organization.

- Identify your external and internal customers.

- Describe effective and ineffective customer-focused behaviors.

- Identify a customer's needs.

- Understand the importance of exceeding customer expectations.

- Understand the importance of regular and proactive communication with a customer.

- Describe the relationship between customer focus and the other Self-Initiated Development competencies.

- Admit mistakes to customers and proactively take steps to remedy a mistake.

- Understand how to better listen to your customers.

- Become an advocate for customers within your organization.

- Model effective customer-focused behaviors to others in your organization.

- Understand each customer's business and their key issues.

- Be perceived as "easy to do business with."

- Understand the importance of meeting deadlines for deliveries to a customer.

Who are Customers?

It is important that we spend a few moments talking about who customers may be. In many cases it is easy to understand who our customers are, and other times it may not be easy. We often find that people who work in administrative areas, such as human resources or procurement, don't realize they have customers, when in reality they do. Here are some things to think about when identifying your customers.

- Customers are often consumers, especially if you are in any type of service industry. These are external (to your organization) customers.

- Customers can be internal to your organization. Internal customers are those who use your products or services as part of doing their job.

- Businesses often have business customers. This relationship may be as simple as one company procuring supplies from another, or as complex as multi-million or billion dollar procurements. If you are a business-to-business organization, everyone in your company should know who your customers are and anyone coming in contact with them either literally or as part of the supplier or service chain should be customer focused.

- Many leaders have both internal and external customers. For example, they may interact with the organization's customers when selling products or services. They may also supply products or services internal to the organization. Leaders must be aware that they must service both constituencies.

Exercise: Who are Customers?

Think of some examples of internal and external customers for each of the following positions.

Airline Pilot	Software Engineer	Football Coach
Financial Manager	School Custodian	University President
Insurance Adjuster	Sales Manager	Quality Manager
Funeral Director	Radiologist	Bank President
Architect	Chief Information Officer	Newspaper Editor

Exercise: Who are YOUR Customers?

Using the space below, list the internal and external customers for your current or aspired position.

INTERNAL CUSTOMERS	EXTERNAL CUSTOMERS

How to Use the Customer Focus Workbook

In the Customer Focus workbook it is critical that you "do the work" to get the most out of it. This section describes each part of the workbook and how to use it to learn more about developing exceptional customer-focused skills and behaviors.

As you proceed through the workbook, remember the SID™ Model and the importance and process of doing your development activities. Your success is dependent on the effort that you put into your development.

Coaches' Orientation

This section introduces and defines customer focus and its importance to a leader. Be sure to read this section first. It also contains a "Coach's Comment." These brief diversions provide you with either an example or personal comment from your coaches.

Customer-focused behaviors

Learning is all about changing behaviors or attitudes. This section includes an exercise to list what you think are effective and ineffective customer-focused behaviors for a leader. We provide our response to this exercise but please do not turn to our response until you have done the best you can do in listing your ideas on effective and ineffective behaviors. After this exercise you will return to reading more text and examples of customer-focused behaviors.

Map Your Growth Exercise

Our Self-Initiated Development (SID™) program is based on thirty competencies, or skills and behaviors grouped into four behavioral categories, found in our 4P's Competency Model. The compass at the beginning of this section shows those that are most related to customer focus. The exercise for this section asks you to describe the relationship between customer focus and each of the related competencies. We then give you our ideas on the relationship.

The Daily Journey

Before continuing your study of customer focus, we present two case study examples, one demonstrating effective customer focus, and the second showing ineffective customer focus. Following each case study you will respond to questions about it (Give Us Your Thoughts). We then provide our responses to each question for you to study (Our Thoughts). This section gives you the opportunity to think further about effective and ineffective customer-focused behaviors.

What Would You Do?

This section provides examples of poor or ineffective customer focus. You are asked to describe what should occur to demonstrate excellent customer-focused behaviors in the situation. Even though some of the examples are "non-business" it is easy to relate the behaviors to your situation. Your Coach then provides thoughts on how the situation should have been handled.

Know Your Heading

Now it is time to do your personal work to improve your customer-focused skills and behaviors. The Know Your Heading section is a brief self assessment of how you view *your* customer-focused skills and behaviors. It is important to be as objective as possible and give thought to each item. The table has a list of statements that you will objectively respond to according to the following options:

1	Strongly Disagree
2	Disagree
3	Agree
4	Strongly Agree
N/A	Not applicable to my current position

You will refer to the number in the PG column for each item later when we discuss specific development recommendations for improvement.

Coaches' Guidance

After your self assessment, it is time to begin thinking of specific behaviors you can change on your road to improvement. This section highlights specific behaviors you can adopt to improve your customer focus.

Coaches' Itinerary

In Part 3 of this workbook you will find the heart of our Self-Initiated Development model with the identification of specific steps that you can take to improve, depending on your score for each statement or item in the Know Your Heading self assessment. In this section, you can do intensive analysis and development planning for each of the assessment items. As your coaches, we provide a starting point for the specific development actions you should follow based on your scores. Follow the instructions at the beginning of the Coaches' Itinerary to review these specific recommendations.

My Development Plan

This is where you create YOUR development plan and build on the information provided in the Coaches' Itinerary to determine what actions you are going to take to improve your customer-focused skills and behaviors. You will also identify what resources you may need to accomplish these actions. Finally, you will assign a realistic date to complete each action.

Takeaway Tools

We provide you with two Takeaway Tools to help improve your skills and behaviors in customer focus. The first is a Customer Focus Worksheet/Checklist. It provides you with guidance on gaining information about customers and directs you through a sequence of steps to identify how you can improve your customer focus with each internal and external customer.

The second Takeaway Tool is an Organizational Customer Focus Assessment. This assessment enables you to gauge how well your organization demonstrates customer focus. You can perform this assessment individually or work with your colleagues.

Coaches' Bookshelf

If you would like to read further about customer focus, we have selected a few of the most relevant books to help you. We have also included a brief commentary on each to help guide your reading selection.

4P's Leadership Competency Model™

The 30 major skills and behaviors (or competencies) that leaders need to demonstrate to sustain effectiveness and success.

Organizational Customer Focus Improvement

We provide general ideas on how to improve overall customer focus at the organizational level using the principles of the SID™ Model.

Summary

We hope the past few pages gave you an idea of how easy this program will be, but at the same time an appreciation for the methods your coaches will use to walk you through each step and improve your customer-focused skills and behaviors. Our goal is that your customer-focused skills and behaviors are improved by using the Development Plan and that you are differentiated from others on your path to success.

"It is not the employer who pays the wages. Employers only handle the money. It is the customer who pays the wages."

- Henry Ford

Coaches' Questions to Ponder

How do you define a "customer?"

How do you define customer focus?

Coaches Orientation

*"Be dramatically willing to focus on the customer
at all costs, even at the cost
of obsoleting your own stuff."*

- Scott Cook

Almost all organizations and leaders have customers. We usually think of customers as those who buy our products or services; however customers can be internal or external. Sometimes those who work in administrative positions with no direct access to an organization's external customers forget that the success of the organization depends on how well they serve their internal customers. For example, a director of Human Resources may not interface with the company's customers, but her customers include all the company's employees, outside vendors, senior leadership, and her peers in other parts of the business. If she is not focused on serving her customers well, their morale may be lower and those who actually interface with the external customers may not do their best job.

Coach's Comment

When we conduct a 360° leadership assessment as part of a coaching program we see dissatisfaction time after time in how the leader responds to or services internal customers. We encourage leaders to set up regular meetings with internal customers to build relationships and get feedback about how they and their team are doing in servicing their internal customers. (Sidney)

Definition

Customer Focus is defined as an individual and organizational orientation toward satisfying the needs of potential and existing internal or external customers.

Importance to an Effective Leader

There is a very simple answer to the question, "Why bother with customer focus?" If you don't focus on existing and potential customers, your business or organization will not achieve its potential, and in fact stands a good chance of failing. Think of restaurants that you may frequent. Some you return to on a regular basis. Others you have visited once and will not return due to poor quality food or inattentive service. Eventually, those businesses that provide poor quality products or services will go out of business.

Leaders determine whether their organization is customer focused or not. Followers emulate the behaviors of leaders, especially when dealing with potential and existing internal or external customers.

Customer-focused behaviors

"We see our customers as invited guests to a party, and we are the hosts. It's our job every day to make every important aspect of the customer experience a little bit better. "

- Jeff Bezos

Customer focus is simple. You need to think about what you can do to meet your customers' needs. Then, take things a step further and ask what more you can do to exceed customer's expectations.

As a leader or aspiring leader, think about what you can do to have an organization that strives hard to please customers. Answer these questions, *"If I ran a competing firm, how would I beat us?"* and *"What would I want from us if I were the customer?"*

Exercise: Customer-focused behaviors

Using the following chart, list what you think are effective and ineffective customer-focused behaviors for leaders.

EFFECTIVE LEADER BEHAVIORS (Customer Focus)	INEFFECTIVE LEADER BEHAVIORS (Customer Focus)

The following table shows our response to the previous reflection exercise. You may have listed additional behaviors. Review this list and think about the behaviors you did not include on your list.

EFFECTIVE LEADER BEHAVIORS (Customer Focus)	INEFFECTIVE LEADER BEHAVIORS (Customer Focus)
• Consistently gives customers more than expected. • Admits mistakes to customers when made and takes steps to fix them. • Consistently meets deadlines for deliveries to customers. • Advocates for customers within their organization. • Strives to provide value to customers. • Proactively identifies customer needs and issues. • Models customer-focused behaviors and rewards those in the organization who are customer focused. • Proactively seeks feedback from customers. • Proactively responds to customer requests. • Seeks to learn and understand the customer's business and industry.	• Ensures that customers only receive what is contractually required. • Does not disclose mistakes to customers and when discovered, attempts to blame others. • Frequently misses deadlines for deliveries to customers. • Strives to "get over" on customers. • Seeks to maximize profit from customers at every step. • Does not strive to learn about customers' needs and issues. • Models non- customer-focused behaviors and rewards those who demonstrate similar behaviors. • Does not seek, nor value, feedback from customers. • Ignores customer requests. • Does not learn about the customer's business or industry.

A Serving Culture: The Petri Dish Where You Meet Your Customer's Needs

What does it mean to be customer focused? Someone once told us that the best account manager is one who wakes up in the morning thinking about what he can do today to improve his customer's business and not what he can do to improve his own business. The theory is that if you do all you can to help your customer's achieve their goals, in the end your company will be successful. There is a lot of truth to this thinking.

Ritz Carlton has built its business model around customer service and focus. From the CEO to the person working in the laundry room, the customer is always first and they actually walk the talk. Ritz Carlton has systems in place to ensure that the customer is always taken care of, but more importantly they live their 12 service values (all directed to delighting the customer). Employees are empowered to engage and take care of customers and any problems that may arise.

If an organization has customer focus as part of its culture, that element plays into how the company develops its strategy, communicates internally and externally, and solves problems. It is up to leaders to ensure that a customer-focus culture works and brings benefit to the customers, the company, and the people. Companies who say they are customer focused must walk the talk; or, very shortly those companies expose themselves for what they are and in fact lose customers. In our workshops, we always say that a company should not say on their brochures or in their proposals that they are customer focused; rather, they should consistently *demonstrate* that they are customer focused. There is nothing worse than saying in a brochure or proposal that you are customer focused and then demonstrate that you are not; a sure way to lose a customer.

Coaches' Motivation

Whenever a person thinks about customer focus they should simply consider, "How would I want to be treated if I were the customer?" The answer is simple – you want to be treated with respect, fairness, and integrity. If you work hard to develop a reputation as being customer focused, you will succeed and go far in your organization.

The Battle for Customer Love

Tactically, what does this mean for leaders? First, leaders need to demonstrate to others in the organization that they are customer focused by always making decisions and solving problems with the customer's interests at the forefront. This does not mean that the customer is always right. It means that the company considers the customer's needs in their decision making process. Leaders must always make the best business decisions for their organization and sometimes this means the customer doesn't walk away with everything they asked for. No matter how absurd it may seem at the outset, the company always considers the customer's needs in the culture of serving others.

Each customer touchpoint within the organization needs to be geared up to interact with customers and learn more about their unique problems, issues, and goals. At every level in your organization, people must realize that without this supreme effort to understand their customer they may miss true service. A customer who feels that he has been truly heard is well on the way to recommending the stellar service he just received to others.

A customer-focus culture also stresses the importance of serving internal customers well. Organizations work better if leaders of departments or teams are aware of what other teams are accomplishing and work to develop good relationships with them. Internal customers are dependent on each other to provide support for projects or to enable the company to function. The better internal customers are serviced, the better external customers are treated.

This is especially true when teams are working on projects that deliver goods or services to customers. Project teams are dependent on many other parts of their organization to get what they need to fulfill their obligations to customers. It is a leader's responsibility to ensure that their teams are working well together within the organization.

The Rubber Meets the Road – Communication

How you communicate with customers is a good example of whether you are customer focused or not. What does a customer think when she never hears from you after you have sold her your product or service? This is a common complaint – once a sale is made the customer never hears from you again. This is foolish behavior on the supplier's part. Communication should continue to ensure that the customer is happy and to determine if there are any more needs to be met.

Think of the messages you and your organization are giving to customers. Do you base your conversations on what the customer's issues may be? Or, do you continually try to "sell?" Build your relationship with a customer by giving them information, helping them solve problems and helping them achieve success.

Consider your customer presentations. Are they customer focused? To be customer focused a presentation should provide the customer with solutions or inform them of the benefits you can provide. Even a sales presentation should not be about you – it should focus on your understanding of the customer's needs and your recommendations for meeting those needs. And, of course, your presentation should be top quality in delivery – dynamic, concise, and of value to the customer.

Reflections on Your Behaviors

Think about your internal and external customers. Rate yourself on how well you service each – poor, adequate, good, excellent. What can you do to improve your service to customers? How do you add value to each?

The Spin Cycle of Value!

Providing value-added information and services at no cost to the customer can be a valuable part of being customer focused. At little or no cost, a customer can receive valuable information or services that help them far beyond what they expect, and they remember you for providing this savings of time and expenditure. As James C. Penney, Founder of J.C. Penney stores once said, "It is the service we are NOT OBLIGED to give that people VALUE the most."

Coach's Comment

Many businesses do not have to advertise; their new business comes from "word of mouth." This is the greatest business builder in the marketplace. When customers voluntarily recommend you, success has been achieved. Even in the largest businesses, customers talk. Word of mouth can be your greatest business builder or it can be your demise. Always think about what your customers may say about you and your organization to other potential customers. (Ben)

Customers also respect your limits and the fact that your company is in business as well. Honesty is the best policy. If you cannot provide something for any reason, be open to the customer about it. This act alone will engender trust and respect between you and the customer.

Your goal in being customer focused is to build a positively differentiated distinction between you and your competition in the customer's mind. This leads to more business for your company and more opportunities to excel at customer focus.

And the cycle of value continues to spin. You add value and the customer will reciprocate by adding value to your company.

The Reciprocal Agreement

Business and customer interactions are reciprocal. We have all seen businesses or some of their employees take their customers for granted and consequently lose customers. Customers **give** something (money) for a product or service and in return expect that product or service to be, at a minimum, as advertised. If they like the product or service, they may be back for more purchases; if they don't like it or can purchase at another business for a better value or experience they will do so. Organizations, on the other hand, **give** something (product or service) in return for the money they receive.

The burden always falls on the selling organization to do their best to satisfy the customer's request in return for the customer's payment and loyalty. Your customer has no responsibility to satisfy your business other than payment for the products or services they purchase. You and your organization have the responsibility to ensure that your customer is satisfied with their purchasing decision.

The Nitty-Gritty

Leaders set the pace for establishing a positive and robust customer-focus culture. There are many details involved in providing and supporting an exceptional customer-focus culture and we cannot possibly cover every aspect for every type of organization and industry; but, we can look at some important basics to build upon in making improvements to your skills and behaviors and the decisions you make for your team or organization.

Here are some important basics for creating delighted and loyal customers:

- **Be Honest** – Of course, we all know "honesty is the best policy." We would like to reframe that quote to say, "Honesty is the ONLY policy." Although it is sometimes tempting to stretch the truth, it is never excusable in the business environment. This applies to advertising your products or services, your brochures, your proposals, and certainly all your individual interactions with your customers, whether face-to-face, phone, or email. Customers can smell things that sound fishy so over communicate if necessary to ensure that your customers understand exactly what they are buying and how it will benefit them.

Don't give customers the opportunity or need to make assumptions about what you are offering. If a customer assumes they will get one thing and you provide something different; problems will almost always ensue.

- **Be Personal** – Buyers want to be respected – always! Customers do not want to feel like a number or that they are interacting with a robot or a detached corporation. How you do this varies depending on your business model and your opportunity to interact with your customers, but make sure that any interaction you have with your customers (online, telephone, or in person) gives positive impressions and attention. As a leader, it is your responsibility to ensure that your organization addresses this aspect in a collaborative manner incorporating sales, operations, and your daily business model.

Coach's Comment

When someone calls your business do they get a "live" person? We once worked with a client that used a recording that required the caller to input the first three letters of the person's name to whom they wanted to talk. A customer could never get a person directly. And, I always wondered, what if you did not know the correct spelling of the person's name? This was truly penny wise, pound foolish. In their desire to save a few dollars by not having a receptionist, they probably lost a lot of business when people gave up trying to reach them. (Ben)

- **Be Professional** – There are few businesses that have loyal and delighted customers without being professional. Gimmicks and out-of-the-box tactics for capturing a customer's attention can be used if carefully implemented and if the audience is appropriate. However, unprofessional behavior is a turn-off and typically damages an organization's credibility. Having a professional face toward the customer builds confidence in the buying decision and develops loyalty. This aspect applies to all communications with customers. If you have one-on-one interactions with customers by phone or face-to-face contact this is especially important. Your appearance, words, and body language all affect how you are perceived and ultimately the customer's final decision to engage with your organization.

- **Be Competent** – How many times have you bought a product or service only to find that it didn't work properly, wasn't installed properly, or didn't take care of our problem or need? How many times have you talked with someone when making a purchasing decision and you were treated rudely or met with a bad attitude? Part of giving exceptional customer focus is the ability to clearly identify a customer's need and provide the correct solution without errors or poor attitude.

  Competence in customer focus not only requires an organization's systems to support quality customer focus, but also the individual skills and behaviors that create exceptional customer interactions. As a leader, you need to determine if your teams need training, tools, or other solutions to provide excellent customer focus. Remember, whoever your "face" to the customer is, that "face" needs to demonstrate competence throughout the cycle of the customer interaction.

Mistakes and Unintended Consequences

Let's begin by asking a question: "Have you ever made a mistake and if so, please raise your hand?" We assume our readers all have their hands raised because at one time or another we have all made mistakes and mistakes typically affect others and perhaps even our credibility. When you make a mistake with a customer *the next thing you do* is vital in maintaining credibility and loyalty. Some immediate actions to mitigate negative consequences if you discover a mistake has taken place include:

- **Acknowledge**. Remember, customers are your livelihood. Don't be shy, defensive, or afraid of the results; immediately acknowledge the mistake and be accountable. The sooner the acknowledgement comes the calmer the customer will react. Customers want to be heard and understood and this need is high if a mistake has been made.

- **Apologize**. Depending on the severity of the mistake, the apology may also vary. Regardless, an immediate apology is mandatory to mitigate negative consequences. If a mistake is extreme or offensive, additional formal apologies may need to take place such as a letter or phone call from a company leader expressing regret and offering to make amends.

- **Answer**. Always respond to a customer calmly. Obviously if you are too calm the customer may not perceive that you care. Be sure to demonstrate a sense of urgency in your response. Do not give excuses; explanations are good, just do not come across with a bad attitude or try to shift blame. Take accountability. Focus on what the customer is saying and be sure you understand the problem or mistake and that your customer believes you understand the situation.

- **Action**. What are you going to do to resolve the situation? If the mistake is complex and you need time to formulate a response, tell the customer you will respond to them within a short period. Be sure to specify the timeframe and ask the best way to contact them. Make sure you keep your word and respond with the actions that you will take to rectify the situation within the promised timeframe. Be sure the customer is satisfied with your actions to correct the mistake.

If you do not resolve mistakes to your customer's satisfaction, the consequences can be severe to you and your organization. We've all heard that an unhappy customer voices their opinion and experience multiple times and word can spread like wildfire especially in our electronic and social media world. Studies have shown that it is over five times more expensive to win a new customer than to aggressively keep a customer. Even after making a mistake, you can aggressively strive to make things right with the customer and ensure that they are a repeat customer. Be a proactive leader in your organization because doing nothing or doing it wrong reaps the negative unintended consequences all leaders should avoid.

Finally, if a mistake has happened with your customer and has been resolved properly and satisfactorily (in their opinion) give some thought to how you can go the extra mile and earn your customer's full trust back and even create a loyal customer out of the unfortunate situation. If necessary, talk to a peer, your team, or your boss. If you can delight your customer after a mistake is resolved it is more likely they will sing your praises than sing of your demise, so go the extra mile!

Deny or Comply?

Once payment for a product or service has been given and the product or service is delivered (hopefully with value and exceptional customer focus), what happens when your customer wants more than you can give? Do you say no, and if so, how do you do it? Or, do you comply?

There is no rule of whether to comply or not. Discretion and courage are attributes needed in formulating and communicating a decision. Begin by asking yourself and perhaps your team or boss the following questions when faced with a difficult decision to deny or comply:

1. Do I truly understand my customer's request and needs? Or, are there underlying and unspoken needs or issues that I need to uncover before making a decision?
2. Is the customer's request reasonable? If so, what are the obstacles to complying with the request?
3. Is the customer being dishonest, unethical, or greedy in their request?
4. Am I too close to the situation and have a bias toward my customer or a personality conflict with my customer?

Having a customer-focus mindset means you go beyond the expected and requested and your focus is about them, not you; remember, you want to delight and create loyalty and repeat business. Of course, your organization needs to stay profitable too, so walking the fine line can periodically be difficult. Here are some tips to help in your decision to deny or comply:

- Be sure you fully understand your customer's request if it goes beyond the ordinary.
- Always check your attitude because we are fallible and sometimes it is best to take a "time-out" or provide your customer with another "face" to your organization that is a better fit.
- If the customer's request is reasonable, comply. Any obstacles you have should be a process of doing business, and perhaps in an improved manner. If you can permanently remove the obstacles by all means, do something permanent.
- Determine how you can negotiate with your customer if the request is too large to approve as requested. Just make sure that the outcome is a win-win.
- If you have to say no, do so in a way that is respectful and gives the customer an understanding of the reason for the decision.

- If the customer is being dishonest, unethical, or taking advantage of you, your position, or your organization, then it is time to take a serious "time-out" and consider how to respond. If this is the case, seek advice from colleagues and your leaders about the best decision for the organization. In some cases, it may be necessary to cease doing business with this type of customer.

Customer Focus and the Connected World

It used to be that we only had to worry about what customers were saying about us to other people in their sphere of influence. Yes, a negative review would hurt but its effect would be limited. We didn't have to worry about things like a web site, blogs, or online comments and reviews.

Today's world is different and the internet and social media add serious responsibilities to our customer focus. Let's consider some of the aspects of the online world and how they can help or hinder (greatly) your customer focus.

Websites

Every company now has a website and it communicates a lot about you and how focused you are in serving those in the marketplace. A good website is essential and is indicative of the quality of products and services you provide. Your website should not only be pleasing to the eye and easy to navigate, but also provide valuable information about your company, your products or services, and topics important to your customers. Here are some good examples:

- Restaurants – We often look up the websites of restaurants we are thinking about visiting. Not only do many restaurant websites provide their hours of operation and directions, but also provide their menus. We can actually think about what we want to order beforehand!

- Universities – Many schools now provide access to student accounts, online records, and course materials. Some offer video tours for prospective students and other features that help them stand out.

- Companies – The best websites for companies include a vast array of information about the organization, its people, and its products and services. Many, however, go beyond this and provide special reports and white papers that their customers may find valuable.

A customer-focused website also may have forums and ways to contact the company "live" to have questions answered or problems solved. Consider how you can use your website to be more customer focused. Review your site in comparison to your competition. How does your site compare?

Internet Review Sites

Today there are sites that enable individuals to review companies, their products, and their services online. Think about how often you may use a review-intensive site, such as Yelp or Travelocity, before dining out or making a hotel reservation. Imagine how destructive it is to a business when a few bad reviews are posted! One bad review can outweigh many, many average or even good reviews.

So, how can Internet review sites help your customer focus? First, and foremost, they can give you an indication of what your customers are saying about you. Sometimes it may be hard to "look in the mirror" but you or someone in your organization should be monitoring review sites. Look for trends, not the isolated negative comment that "comes from left field." After your analysis, consider the comments and what you can do about them. Hopefully, you will receive excellent feedback and any that is negative will describe specific situations that you can act upon.

Facebook, Linkedin, Google+

Many organizations are beginning to use Facebook, originally designed for social networking, as a method to promote their company and provide customer service. Your organization's Facebook page can be very similar to a website and offer links to your main site, opportunities to interact with customers, and the ability to provide promotions and special offers.

Linkedin is designed to connect professionals. It was originally developed to help professionals and companies "link up" to learn employment opportunities. However, it has also expanded and there are "groups" of people with similar interests and connections with organization. People (you or your customer, for example) can write entries or blogs to your group. For example, we have created a Linkedin group for customer focus. If you are a Linkedin member (or join now) you can join our group at: http://www.linkedin.com/groups/Customer-Focus-SelfInitiated-Development-3795487?trk=myg_ugrp_ovr. As with most groups, content is updated frequently and you can post your own comments or blogs.

Google+ is a new endeavor designed by Google to compete with Facebook. It will be unique because you will be able to interact with and engage your clients by putting them in "circles." Google+ is still in its testing phase and it is unclear what the complete set of features will be; however, their promotion campaign states that it will be the "Facebook" for professionals.

These sites are additional opportunities to engage and provide service to your customers. It is important to note that, as with any interaction with customers, they must look professional, offer value for the reader's time, and give information that customers can use in their business. Social media is more than a passing fad – it is here to stay. But, it can be abused and a great time waster if not used for engaging your colleagues and customers.

What are YOUR Customers Saying?

In the last section we introduced you to new ways that customers have to tell you (and the world!) what you are doing well and what you need to improve. Now, let's take it a step further.

Do you know how well you are doing with your customers? The first step is to assess your own skills and behaviors in this area which is found in the "Know Your Heading" section of this workbook. After you have completed this exercise, the second step is to understand how customer focused your organization's culture supports your goals in this area. A starting place for this exercise is found in Takeaway Tool 2 in Appendix B of this workbook. With these data points, you have needed information to narrow your focus on the best starting points to implement improvements in your personal skills and behaviors and for needed organizational culture changes.

Last, but not least, is validating your focus prior to any major *organizational* changes by asking your customers and internal staff to rate your products and services. As a leader, if you are serious about providing exceptional customer focus then this component should not be overlooked. Not only will your customers know you care about them, but your employees will also recognize that you value their input and expertise.

One of the best places to start within your own organization is by surveying your employees on gaps they have experienced or observed in providing excellent customer focus. This should include internal customer interactions and processes as well as gaining their perceptions of external customer focus. In the majority of cases when internal employees are surveyed in this manner, they are able to identify specific issues that create roadblocks to successfully providing exceptional customer focus.

Surveying customers has become standard in almost every industry and as consumers we see this almost every time we make a purchase. There are many methods to gather data from your customers and the methodology used should fit your business, whether it is by having your staff contact people and ask for the data, hiring an external firm, or implementing an online option to gather this data.

The point is to periodically gather data from your buyers and then DO something about this data to continuously improve your customer focus. After taking actions to improve, communicate these actions to your customers so they know you take their concerns seriously.

Finally, as a leader in your organization, customer focus starts with you. We cannot restate this enough. If you are leading by example you are showing others how it is achieved and that exceptional behaviors in customer focus are a priority.

Map Your Growth

Customer focus is related to a number of other competencies in our 4P's Leadership Competency Model™. It is important to understand the relationship between customer focus and the related competencies. For example, if influencing skills are a weakness for you, creating a culture in your organization that is customer focused will be more difficult.

Below we show the most relevant leadership competencies within our 4P's Competency Model™ to customer focus and beginning on the next page, is a chart for you to describe the relationship between each competency and customer focus. For example, what impact does this competency have on your customer-focused behaviors? There is no "right" or "wrong" answer. Our description of the relationships begins on page 48.

Customer Focus Related Leadership Competencies

Persuasive Vision

Influencing
Planning
Strategic Thinking

People Skills

Communications
Interpersonal Skills
Negotiation
Problem Solving

Positive Results

Business Development
Commitment to Quality
Decision Making

Personal Character

Credibility
Followership
Initiative
Integrity
Trust

COMPETENCY	RELATIONSHIP TO CUSTOMER FOCUS

Persuasive Vision

Influencing	
Planning	
Strategic Thinking	

Positive Results

Business Development	
Commitment to Quality	
Decision Making	

COMPETENCY	RELATIONSHIP TO CUSTOMER FOCUS

Personal Character

Credibility	
Followership	
Initiative	
Integrity	
Trust	

People Skills

Communications	
Interpersonal Skills	
Negotiation	
Problem Solving	

COMPETENCY	RELATIONSHIP TO CUSTOMER FOCUS

Persuasive Vision

Influencing	Influencing is the practice of convincing others to think the way you do or to take an action. If you are customer focused you will need to influence your customers and also your internal organization (to be more customer focused).
Planning	Your organization should develop plans describing how they will be customer focused. You can plan activities that involve customers or develop messages that you want communicated to customers.
Strategic Thinking	For your organization to be perceived as being customer focused, it is critical that you develop long-term strategies that emphasize your organization's customer-focus strategy.

Positive Results

Business Development	If you are not customer focused your business development activities will suffer. For your organization to prosper and grow, your business development activities must prove to your potential customers that you have a customer-focus culture.
Commitment to Quality	Quality is important to your customers. Demonstrate that you are customer focused by providing flawless quality to your customers. If you make a mistake, admit it and make it up to the customer.
Decision Making	When making decisions it is important to consider the impact on your customers. Although it is important to make decisions in the best interests of your organization, it is important to consider the impact on customers because that produces the long-term effect on your organization.

COMPETENCY	RELATIONSHIP TO CUSTOMER FOCUS
Personal Character	
Credibility	It is important to establish and maintain credibility with your customers. Always do what you say you will do for customers. If you have the opportunity to exceed their expectations, don't hesitate.
Followership	Following the direction of your organization's customer-focus goals and standards create a culture for positive customer-focused behaviors.
Initiative	It takes work to be customer focused. Effective leaders take the initiative to not only be customer focused themselves but also to develop a customer-focus culture in their organization.
Integrity	Leaders must always be aware of how they are communicating and demonstrating their integrity to customers. Always tell the truth to customers and seek to always be as transparent as possible.
Trust	If customers trust you and your organization they will want to work with you. It takes work and integrity to build trust. Be careful not to damage trust with a customer.

COMPETENCY	RELATIONSHIP TO CUSTOMER FOCUS

People Skills

Communications	Your effectiveness and adaptability in communications with customers are a large part of demonstrating your customer focus.
Interpersonal Skills	To be customer focused you need to "get along" with customers. Your interpersonal skills contribute by helping customers realize that they want to get along with you and work with you.
Negotiation	Negotiations can always be an opportunity to demonstrate your customer focus. However, if, during negotiations, you demonstrate that you are concerned about your customer's position and their success, your customer focus is highlighted.
Problem Solving	If problems occur between your organization and a customer, how you solve the problem can demonstrate your customer focus, build trust, and further the relationship. Work with customers to solve problems.

The Daily Journey

Every organization should strive to ensure that their employees are customer focused. Consider the following case study:

Chicken Soup for the Customer's Soul

While doing a workshop I ended up at a very bad hotel. Not only was the room horrible, there were illicit and loud activities going on all over the place! I made the mistake of eating in the restaurant and by midnight, I was in the throes of terrible food poisoning. Bottom line, I got no sleep and was still feeling terrible at 8:00 the next morning.

I went to the front desk to get a late checkout so I could try to sleep. The front desk clerk seemed to take pleasure in informing me of their policy, "We don't offer late checkout." I explained the situation and pleaded for just a few hours to recover. She said, even more pompously, "We don't ever do any late checkout – period."

I packed my clothes and managed to drive to the north end of the city where I had a meeting the next day with another client. I had a reservation at a Marriott hotel and was pleased that I was moving up in the world.

When I walked into the hotel the front desk clerk asked, "Are you alright? You look ill."

I could barely choke out my reply, "I'm OK. I've just been up all night with food poisoning."

Immediately, she told me to go to my room. "You can come down later and sign the register, sir. Don't worry about it right now." Then she handed me the room key and I started to hobble away. Suddenly, I heard my name and caught the concerned look in her I as I turned, weak and bleary-eyed.

"Mr. McDonald, I know you are very tired and not feeling well; but, please don't go to sleep for at least ten minutes."

My thoughts were, sure – whatever.

A few minutes after settling into my very nice room, I heard a knock on the door. When I opened it there was a man standing with a bowl of the most delicious smelling chicken soup and a sparkling glass of ginger ale. I was a bit taken aback and he said with a friendly smile, "This is compliments of Judy at the front desk and I hope you feel better." He refused my offer to pay and assured me the gift was compliments of Judy. Besides, he explained, "Chicken soup isn't even on our menu so I wouldn't even know what to charge!"

GIVE US YOUR THOUGHTS!

- Do you think I recounted this story, using the names of the hotels, to many people since it occurred? How have similar situations (positive and negative) affected your business?

- How would you have rewarded the front desk clerk at the Marriott?

- What were the specific behaviors the Marriott clerk used that demonstrated customer focus?

- What kind of training do you believe was implemented at the Marriott that resulted in my bowl of chicken soup? How productive was the rigid stance of management at the original hotel? What do you think the long-term result will be for this hotel?

- Do you think that my "frugal" client was adding value to servicing his internal customers by saving money on my lodging?

For our thoughts on the questions about this case study, turn to the next page. Our thoughts are not necessarily the "right answers." Your responses on the previous page may be excellent and add an additional perspective on the questions. The important thing is that you think each question through and give your best response.

Coaches' Questions to Ponder

Have you had a similar experience? If so, what did you do?

OUR THOUGHTS!

- Do you think I recounted this story, using the names of the hotels, to many people since it occurred? How have similar situations (negative or positive) affected your business?

  Yes, many times. When people have very bad experiences (and excellent ones) they typically tell many people about the experiences. This can have a profound effect on your business and/or personal reputation. As a leader you need to develop a culture that is aware that every person's behaviors can have an effect on the long-term health of the business.

- How would you have rewarded the front desk clerk at the Marriott?

  As a consumer, always look for ways to reward those who provide excellent service. The first step may be to talk with the person's manager to explain the situation and relate how the person handled it. A personal letter to the hotel manager would be another method of ensuring that the excellent behaviors were recognized.

- What were the specific behaviors the Marriott clerk used that demonstrated customer focus?

  She demonstrated immediate concern for my well being. She expedited the check in process so that I may get to my room as soon as possible. She ordered the chicken soup quickly so I would be able to go to sleep within minutes of arrival.

- What kind of training do you believe was implemented at the Marriott that resulted in my bowl of chicken soup? How productive was the rigid stance of management at the original hotel? Their employee followed the rules at what cost?

  It is obvious that the Marriott hotel trains its employees on how to please customers and gives them the latitude to behave outside the box. The first hotel did not place any emphasis on customer service. By not being flexible in meeting my needs, the hotel received a lot of negative publicity and lost the contract with my client for future workshops. This incident cost them thousands of dollars!

- Do you think that my "frugal" client was adding value to servicing his internal customers by saving money on my lodging?

  My client was not treating his internal customers (employees and consultants) well and this attitude was manifested in my not being able to deliver the second day of the workshop. In addition, by my client looking for the most inexpensive accommodations, participants were put at risk and the training was not as conducive as possible for learning. In the long term, fewer managers and leaders would take advantage of the training offered by the company because they knew the conditions would be stressful.

To improve, it is good to analyze examples of poor customer focus. Consider the following case study:

Sit Down – I Have the Floor!

I recall years ago that I was consulting with a company that was submitting a proposal for a training system to a large technology company. We were clearly the frontrunner and were confident that we would be chosen. Before selection we were invited to the company to make a presentation to the Senior Vice President and his staff about our proposal. This was typical and did not concern us; being a method that companies use to determine if they could work with us.

At the beginning of the meeting the Senior Vice President stated clearly that he had another meeting at exactly 1:30 and we needed to be finished by then. No problem! We walked through our presentation and handed off to our Vice President of Sales at about 1:00 for a summary and questions and answers.

We were surprised when our Vice President restarted the presentation from the beginning – hopefully he was not going to go through everything again! But, he was. As the clock ticked closer to 1:30 we could see that the Senior Vice President was checking his watch. At about 1:25 he reminded us that he needed to leave at 1:30. "No problem," said our Vice President.

At 1:29 the Senior Vice President began to get up from his chair. To our amazement, our Vice President said, "Please sit down. I am not finished yet." A few minutes later he began to get up from his chair again and was rudely told to sit down again. Meanwhile, we were trying to signal our Vice President to end and sit down himself, to no avail.

Finally, at 1:35 the Senior Vice President stood up and said, "I must leave now for my meeting. You will hear from us shortly." As we watched him and his team file from the room we were filled with fear and the inevitability of a sure loss. Our Vice President looked at us and said, "Well, that was rude of him to just leave. I'm not sure we should work with these idiots anyway."

By the time we were back at our office the next morning we had received the phone call that we would not be considered for the work.

GIVE US YOUR THOUGHTS!

- Were we overconfident?

- What should our Vice President of Sales have done during the last half hour of our presentation?

- Why do you think we lost, even though we were clearly the most qualified company to submit a bid for the project?

- What are some standards you can think of to ensure that customer focus is demonstrated in a meeting?

- What do you think happened to our Vice President of Sales?

- Were others on our team also partly responsible?

For our thoughts on the questions about this case study, turn to the next page. Our thoughts are not necessarily the "right answers." Your responses on the previous page may be excellent and add an additional perspective on the questions. The important thing is that you think each question through and give your best response.

Coaches' Questions to Ponder

Have you had a similar experience? If so, what did you do?

OUR THOUGHTS!

- Were we overconfident?

  Yes, most likely we were. We did not view the meeting as being a major factor in the company's decision. If we had, we would have practiced the presentation repeatedly and ensured that the Vice President handled the ending in a customer-focused manner.

- What should our Vice President of Sales have done during the last half hour of our presentation?

  He should have briefly summarized and then opened the meeting to questions from the customer. He could have reviewed the customer's issues and demonstrated that he knew what their problem was and how we were going to help them solve it.

- Why do you think we lost, even though we were clearly the most qualified company to submit a bid for the project?

  Customers want to know if they can work with you and that you respect them and are concerned about their growth and success. The Vice President's behavior did not make us seem appealing to work with. Customers would rather work with someone who may be slightly less qualified but easy to work with than arrogant people and organizations.

- What are some standards you can think of to ensure that customer focus is demonstrated in a meeting?

  - *Focus on the customer's issues*
  - *Obey the rules established up front regarding time and agenda*
  - *Summarize and open the floor to questions*
  - *Practice any customer presentation*

- What do you think happened to our Vice President of Sales?

  He was subsequently fired.

- Were others on our team also partly responsible?

  Yes, especially those of us who were more experienced. We could have found a way to interrupt our Vice President in such a way that neither the customer would have been disturbed nor our Vice President would not have lost face in the situation. We should have insisted on practicing the presentation before the meeting.

What Would You Do?

Instructions

The following are examples of poor customer-focused behaviors. After each behavior, describe what should occur to demonstrate excellent customer focus.

1. Insurance agents who call or visit you weekly until you sign for a new policy. Then you never hear from them again – until your heirs try to cash in the policy.

2. A company that promises everything in a proposal – and delivers – but only because they are contractually obligated to do so. In addition, getting every promise fulfilled is like pulling teeth from an alligator.

3. Driving employees to get the most for the least from vendors.

4. Self-service gasoline pumps – remember when you were able to get gas for 80% less cost, had your oil checked and windshield cleaned?

5. The expectation to give a tip at a coffee bar when the barista only poured your coffee (big jar labeled TIPS!).

6. Sending an e-mail to a company with a request and never getting a response.

7. Calling a company and getting a recording; then being asked to enter the first three digits of the last name of the person you want to talk with. How do I know to whom I want to talk? Moreover, how do I spell their name?

8. Calling an agency to ask about the whereabouts of a check that is overdue and having the person tell you (with a laugh), "We are behind almost six weeks in cutting checks. We only have one supervisor to sign checks and she is on vacation for two weeks (ha ha)."

Exercise

Add any examples of poor customer focus or service that you have experienced.

Your Coaches' Thoughts

The following are our thoughts about each of these poor customer-focused behaviors. Compare to your thoughts on the previous pages.

1. Insurance agents who call or visit you weekly until you sign for a new policy. Then you never hear from them again – until your heirs try to cash in the policy.

   Good customer focus would consist of the agent contacting you on a regular basis after you sign for the new policy. This would enable them to build a relationship with you, learn more about your needs, and be prepared to offer changes to your policy should the situation warrant. This could also include sending birthday and holiday greetings. The customer's reaction in this example would be to likely go to another company when the policy was up for renewal.

2. A company that promises everything in a proposal – and delivers – but only because they are contractually obligated to do so. In addition, getting every promise fulfilled is like pulling teeth from an alligator.

   Companies that win a project should fulfill their obligations and more; and they should do this without making it difficult for the customer. Customer-focused companies are proactive and flexible in meeting a customer's needs and exceeding their expectations.

3. Driving employees to get the most for the least from vendors.

   Treat vendors like business partners. Companies should treat their vendors well and they will get excellent treatment in return. Vendors who feel beaten down by their clients tend to do less quality work and hesitate to add value to what they are doing for the client.

4. Self-service gasoline pumps – remember when you were able to get gas for 80% less cost, had your oil checked and windshield cleaned?

   Imagine the increase in business that a gas station would get if it provided more than self-service gasoline. Do you think people would pay a few cents per gallon more if they knew they would be able to get their gas pumped, oil checked, and windshield washed?

5. The expectation to receive a tip at a coffee bar when the barista only poured your coffee (big jar labeled TIPS!).

   Customers are to provide tips when the server or attendant provides extra service, not as a routine matter in many situations. The barista at the coffee bar is getting a better salary than a restaurant server is, and should not expect a tip except in extraordinary circumstances.

6. Sending an e-mail to a company with a request and never receiving a response.

   Companies should respond to e-mail correspondence as quickly as possible, even if it is simply a response acknowledging receipt of the customer's mail and the promise to get back to them within a reasonable time.

7. Calling a company and getting a recording; then being asked to enter the first three letters of the last name of the person you want to talk with. How do I know to whom I want to talk? Moreover, how do I spell their name?

   Companies should always have a human voice answering phone calls to their general number. An exception could be made for a number with a specific purpose that is designed to route callers to a specific department. The customer's perception when a recording answers a general number would never be good. The customer may assume that the company is struggling financially and cannot afford someone dedicated to answering the phone. Most, however, will simply hang up and call the competition.

8. Calling an agency to asking for the whereabouts of a check that is overdue and having the person tell me (with a laugh), "We are behind almost six weeks in cutting checks. We only have one supervisor to sign checks and she is on vacation for two weeks (Ha! Ha!)"

   Laughing at someone's financial inquiry is very insensitive. The agency should show empathy and demonstrate that they are proactive in solving the problem. The customer's reaction to the person laughing would be frustration.

Know Your Heading

Now that you have a better understanding of customer focus and its associated behaviors, it is time to self assess your current behaviors. To focus your future development activities and achieve your goals, it is important that you be reflective and honest in completing your self assessment. As you reflect on each statement, consider how others would respond as well. Think about how others perceive your behavior related to each statement. For example, if your primary customers are external, think of some as you complete your scoring. If your primary customers are internal, use them as your frame of reference.

Instructions: Read each of the skills and behaviors below. As objectively as possible, score yourself for each according to the following scale: 1 = strongly disagree; 2 = disagree; 3 = agree; 4 = strongly agree. If a behavior is not appropriate for your position or aspired position, check the N/A column.

The PG column indicates the page number for a deeper discussion of development recommendations for each behavioral statement. Later you will refer to these pages to help you complete your development action plan.

SKILL OR BEHAVIOR	1	2	3	4	N/A	PG
I consistently strive to delight customers by giving more than expected.						78
I admit my mistakes and take steps to "fix" them.						82
I consistently meet deadlines for deliveries to customers.						86
I advocate for customers within my organization.						90
I strive to provide value to customers.						94
I am proactive in identifying customer needs and issues.						98
I model customer-focused behaviors.						102

SKILL OR BEHAVIOR	1	2	3	4	N/A	PG
I proactively seek feedback from customers and listen to their comments.						106
I proactively respond to customer requests.						110
I seek to understand my customer's key issues.						114
I am "easy to do business with."						118
I follow through with what I commit to a customer.						122

Scoring

Review your score for each item. Based on your score for an item, follow the directions below:

- Read the Coaches' Guidance beginning on the next page. Regardless of your score, this section will provide valuable tips to improve your customer-focused skills and behaviors.

- For each item, especially those in which you scored a (1) strongly disagree or (2) disagree, refer to the developmental recommendations page in the Coaches' Itinerary section for that item. Read and consider the recommendations for that item.

Coaches' Guidance

> ### *Coach's Comment*
> *You are a customer in many ways – buying an automobile, eating at a restaurant, traveling – and you expect excellent customer focus. Why shouldn't your customers expect the same? (Ben)*

Now that you have taken the self assessment to gain an understanding of the behaviors that are your strengths and weaknesses in customer focus, consider the following general recommendations.

- **Do what is not expected – for both external and internal customers.** Doing something extra or special is not difficult and customers remember this for a long time. Think about what customers expect and then decide what you can do for them that is "above and beyond." For example, for an external customer, if you see something on the internet that would benefit their business, such as an opportunity to speak at a conference in their field, send it to them. For an internal customer, provide what is needed and then personally follow up to see if there is more that you can do to help them.

- **Try not to make mistakes; but if you do, turn them into opportunities.** If you do make a mistake, admit it, fix it, and demonstrate an attitude that shows you care and will do what is right. Customers appreciate honesty and transparency and you have an opportunity to turn a negative into a positive.

- **Treat your employees as if they are customers.** This models the behaviors you expect them to extend to your customers. Primarily, this means that you need to fulfill your commitments and promises to them. If you tell an employee that you will talk with them later that day, do not forget. And, when they come to meet with you, genuinely show interest in what they have to say. Do not rush the meeting and set the time aside strictly for them.

- **Be proactive in dealing with customers; foresee their needs and address them before asked.** Being proactive is an opportunity to demonstrate how good you are. If you put yourself in the customer's shoes and know their customers and marketplace it is much easier to anticipate ways to help them. Customers love people who bring something to their attention they are not aware of or give them ideas on how to improve their business. This works well with internal customers as well. If you have an idea that will help an internal customer, bring it to their attention.

- **Be "easy" to do business with.** Give the customer the perception that you are friendly and will bend over backward to take care of them. This is especially true after you have them as a customer. It is easy to treat a potential customer well and then forget about them after you have made the sale. The best companies treat their customers just as well or better after they have made the sale. If there are obstacles or issues that need to be overcome, work with the customer to find the win-win solution. Be pleasant and not adversarial.

- **Be an advocate for your customer within your organization.** Often a company makes decisions that affect customers without considering the ramifications to the customer and the potential negative long-term effect to the relationship. If you work closely with a customer you have a perspective on how your organization's decisions can affect them. Bring this perspective to light and work toward decisions that will have minimal negative effect on customers.

- **Follow through with what you say.** If you make a promise or commitment, keep it. Never fail in this area; it will cost you a customer and damage your organization's reputation.

- **Focus on your customer, not your operation.** Sometimes it is more appropriate to please a customer than to follow all the rules. This does not mean that you circumvent rules that can impact how you do business with other customers; rather it means that you should do all that you can do to please the customer and if you need to ignore a rule that has minimal impact within your organization to deliver outstanding service and care, and then do so.

- **Listen to your customers.** You may have formal means to get customer feedback, such as a survey. But, it is even more useful to ask them for feedback in person. After you have listened, take action on their concerns and follow-up with them to give the status. If you cannot do anything about a concern, tell them. Customers will appreciate your honesty. This is an excellent strategy to use with internal customers as well. Take the time to listen to those who are internal customers. Ask them for feedback on how well you service them.

- **Take the attitude that complaints are gifts and problems are opportunities – but only if you act on them.** Acting on complaints from customers is top priority. After you have corrected the situation, be sure to tell the customer what you have done and the steps you have taken to ensure that it will not happen again. If the customer complains about something you cannot change, explain why you cannot change the situation and ask for their suggestions on how things could be done better.

- **Teach others how to be customer focused.** It is all about focusing on the customer, not the operation. Sam Walton, founder of WalMart said, *"There is only one boss – the customer. Customers can fire everybody in the company, from the Chairman on down, simply by spending their money somewhere else."*

- **Be responsive.** If you tell a customer you will do something within the next two days, do it within the next few hours. If a customer has a problem that seriously affects their business, drop everything to do what you can to help resolve the problem; do not just put it on your schedule.

"When every physical and mental resource is focused, one's power to solve a problem multiplies tremendously."
- Norman Vincent Peale

Coaches' Questions to Ponder

Are you ready to concentrate intently on improving your customer focus?

How much time do you have available each week to devote to professional improvement?

Are you satisfied with the scores you gave yourself on the Know Your Heading self assessment?

Part 3 – Development Resources and Appendices

Coaches' Itinerary

In this section you can do intensive analysis and development planning for each of the items in the self assessment for Customer Focus. We recommend that you specifically focus on those items that you scored yourself a 1 (strongly disagree) or 2 (disagree) in the Know Your Heading exercise (page 63) and create a development plan based on the recommendations for those items. We also urge that you review the recommendations for items that you scored a 3 (agree) or 4 (strongly agree) and learn more how you can emphasize a strength or work toward creating a culture of customer focus in your organization.

I consistently strive to delight customers by giving more than expected.

Your Coaches' Comments About This Item

Think about how you feel when you get more than you expected as a customer. You feel very good about it – you received a bargain, you were treated well, and most likely you will tell others about your experience.

Giving customers more than they expect is a mindset. You need to be thinking about it all the time and being proactive in making it happen. You can't always give the customer more than he or she expects, but your behaviors and attitude may be what exceeds their expectations.

Coach's Challenge

I hate shopping for a new car. To me it is a very difficult experience and always feel that I am being taken advantage of...even if I may like the sales person. I don't expect much, but if the dealer is friendly and not too "salesy" I begin to feel better. Then, if the sales person truly listens to me, seems to be concerned about my needs, and bends a few rules to give me what I want, I feel really good and it turns into a much better experience.

Think about similar situations you have been in where a sales person or other company representative made you feel comfortable.

On the next two pages, circle the score you gave yourself for this statement in the Know Your Heading exercise on page 71 for this statement. Then, read the Coaches' Recommendations for your score.

"The first step in exceeding your customer's expectations is to know those expectations."
- Roy H. Williams

I consistently strive to delight customers by giving more than expected.

Your Score: 1 (strongly disagree) 2 (disagree) 3 (agree) 4 (strongly agree)

Score: 1	Coaches' Recommendations

You feel that you could significantly improve in this area. Ask yourself the following questions:

- Why do I not strive to delight customers by giving them more than expected?

- What are the obstacles to giving my customers more than expected?

Use the Takeaway Tools for this competency in Appendices A and B to identify your internal and external customers. List each customer's expectations for you. If you do not know their expectations, speak with them to learn how you can meet and exceed their expectations.

Score: 2	Coaches' Recommendations

You feel you can improve in this area. Typically, we feel we can only give the customer what they are paying for and nothing more. This is not the case. Often, you can provide more value or value-added deliverables to a customer at little or no cost.

What are the results of giving a customer more than expected?

Use the Takeaway Tools for this competency in Appendices A and B to identify your internal and external customers. List each customer's expectations for you. If you do not know their expectations, speak with them to learn how you can meet and exceed their expectations.

I consistently strive to delight customers by giving more than expected.

Your Score: 1 (strongly disagree) 2 (disagree) 3 (agree) 4 (strongly agree)

Score: 3	Coaches' Recommendations

This is a good score but there is room for improvement. Search for more opportunities to delight customers by giving them more than expected.

Use the Takeaway Tools for this competency in Appendices A and B to identify your internal and external customers. List each customer's expectations for you. If you do not know their expectations, speak with them to learn how you can meet and exceed their expectations.

Score: 4	Coaches' Recommendations

This is an excellent score for this item. Continue to give customers more than expected. Look for opportunities to encourage others to do the same in your organization.

Think about how you can create a culture in your organization that "under-promises and over-delivers." Reward team members who work to delight customers. Do not tolerate those in the organization who try to "get over" on a customer.

I consistently strive to delight customers by giving more than expected.

List the development steps will you take to improve in this item.

1.

2.

3.

4.

Other Notes:

I admit my mistakes and take steps to "fix" them.

Your Coaches' Comments About This Item

The essence of this item is not that we should be perfect and never make mistakes; rather, it is what we do after we make a mistake that is important. You will make mistakes.

Far too often when mistakes are made they lead to finger pointing and blame games. Even when it is obvious who made the error and how it happened. It seems to always be someone else's fault.

Be different. If you make a mistake, take responsibility for it. Do what you need to do to fix the effects of the mistake. Be honest with your customer. Tell them what you will be doing to correct the mistake and minimize the impact.

Coach's Challenge

Have you made a mistake lately? Probably. If you have, what do you need to do? Do you need to take steps to fix any effects of the mistake? Do you need to talk to a colleague or customer to explain the mistake you made and what you intend to do about it?

On the next two pages, circle the score you gave yourself for this statement in the Know Your Heading exercise on page 71 for this statement. Then, read the Coaches' Recommendations for your score.

"The only man who never makes a mistake is the man who never does anything."

- Theodore Roosevelt

I admit my mistakes and take steps to "fix" them.

Your Score: 1 (strongly disagree) 2 (disagree) 3 (agree) 4 (strongly agree)

Score: 1	Coaches' Recommendations

You indicate that you need significant improvement in this area. It is important to recognize when a mistake is made and to atone for it and take steps to fix the problem or ensure that it will not happen again.

Don't try to hide mistakes from customers. When the reality is exposed they will not appreciate your deception. It is important to be honest and up front with customers when you make a mistake; you can even turn a mistake into an opportunity to strengthen the relationship.

Think of mistakes you have made in the past. What could you have done differently to prevent the mistake? What could you have done after recognizing the mistake to minimize the damage to the relationship with your customer?

Score: 2	Coaches' Recommendations

To improve in this area you need to first recognize when you make a mistake. Think about what you could have done to prevent the mistake; then, determine how you will rectify the situation.

Many customers appreciate it when their interactions are transparent with others. In fact, being honest about mistakes, along with concrete steps to make amends, can improve the relationship rather than damage it.

Think of mistakes you have made in the past. What could you have done differently to prevent the mistake? What could you have done after recognizing the mistake to minimize the damage to the relationship with your customer?

I admit my mistakes and take steps to "fix" them.

Your Score: 1 (strongly disagree)   2 (disagree)   3 (agree)   4 (strongly agree)

Score: 3	Coaches' Recommendations

This is a good score for this item, but consider why you do not strongly agree. Have you made too many mistakes? If so, slow down and think about causes for the mistakes. Were you too busy or stressed to make a good decision? Were you swayed by other influences?

Think about strategies you can use to repair your relationships with a customer when you make a mistake. What steps will you take to not only repair, but also strengthen the relationship because of the situation?

Refer to the Individual Takeaway Tool in Appendix A.

Score: 4	Coaches' Recommendations

Excellent score for this item. Continue to model this behavior.

Review the organizational assessment Takeaway Tool in Appendix B. How well does your organization do in this area? Are there people in your organization that make too many mistakes? Are there people who attempt to hide mistakes from customers? If so, as a leader, it is your responsibility to change this culture.

Emphasize to your direct reports and others in the organization that it is important to recognize mistakes and be transparent to the customer. When mistakes are made, always consider the steps you need to take to be honest with the customer and rebuild the relationship.

I admit my mistakes and take steps to "fix" them.

List the development steps will you take to improve in this item.

1.

2.

3.

4.

Other Notes:

I consistently meet deadlines for deliveries to customers.

Your Coaches' Comments About This Item

Sometimes there must be a tradeoff between quality and the deadline. We can always make things better, but is that the right thing to do if we don't make the deadline? High-technology companies realize that they must be the "first to market" for their products, sometimes at the expense of quality. Yes, the product must work and do what the company is promising, but the bells and whistles can come later. Most of the time, meeting the deadline is more important that perfect quality. Leaders realize this and work to maximize quality and still meet the deadline.

Coach's Challenge

Have you ever encountered someone who always strived to make something better and it was never quite good enough (in their eyes) to deliver to a customer? What do you as a leader do in this situation? You have a deadline for a delivery to the customer, the product meets the customer's expectations, but someone is dragging their feet because they are not satisfied yet? How do you handle the situation, meet the deadline, and maintain the dignity of the person who is striving to make the product even better?

On the next two pages, circle the score you gave yourself for this statement in the Know Your Heading exercise on page 71 for this statement. Then, read the Coaches' Recommendations for your score.

"Crystallize your goals. Make a plan for achieving them and set yourself a deadline. Then, with supreme confidence, determination and disregard for obstacles and other people's criticisms; carry out your plan."
- Paul J. Meyer

I consistently meet deadlines for deliveries to customers.

Your Score: 1 (strongly disagree) 2 (disagree) 3 (agree) 4 (strongly agree)

Score: 1	Coaches' Recommendations

It is imperative that deadlines are met. You feel that you do not consistently meet delivery deadlines.

It is important to recognize why you are missing deadlines. It is critical that you be honest with yourself and not blame others (unless deserved). Think about the reasons for missing deadlines. What prevented you from achieving the deadline? What could you have done differently?

One technique is to set an artificial deadline a comfortable period of time before the actual deadline. Plan to have the work completed by the early deadline; that way the deliverable is completed before needed.

Score: 2	Coaches' Recommendations

It is important that deadlines are consistently met for customer deliveries. You feel you need to improve in this area. Perhaps there are external reasons for not meeting deadlines. What can you do to ensure that you have the time and resources needed to meet all deadlines?

If there is a problem with your organization's structure or processes that leads to deadlines being missed, as a leader you have a responsibility to take steps to fix the problem.

Think about how you can change any obstacles in your organization to ensure that every deadline is met.

I consistently meet deadlines for deliveries to customers.

Your Score: 1 (strongly disagree) 2 (disagree) 3 (agree) 4 (strongly agree)

Score: 3	Coaches' Recommendations

It is important that deadlines are consistently met for customer deliveries. You feel you do well in this area but there is some room to improve. Perhaps there are external reasons for not meeting deadlines. What can you do to ensure that you have the time and resources needed to meet all deadlines?

Assess how well others on your team meet deadlines. Is your organization getting a bad reputation with a customer because of missed deadlines? If so, be proactive to work with others to meet deadlines.

Refer to the organizational customer focus assessment Takeaway Tool in Appendix B and use it to help determine any problem areas.

Score: 4	Coaches' Recommendations

Congratulations. This is an excellent score and indicates that you do not miss customer deadlines. However, as a leader, you should look around the organization and assess whether any of your colleagues have a problem in this area. Your organization's reputation can be damaged significantly by one missed deadline.

Refer to the organizational customer focus assessment Takeaway Tool in Appendix B and use it to help determine any problem areas.

I consistently meet deadlines for deliveries to customers.

List the development steps will you take to improve in this item.

1.

2.

3.

4.

Other Notes:

I advocate for customers within my organization.

Your Coaches' Comments About This Item

It can be difficult to be an advocate for your clients or customers within your own organization. Sometimes your loyalty may be questioned. But, if you are transparent about your advocacy and how it is important for your organization to consider customers in their decisions and changes, the benefits will be clear to others.

To be an effective advocate you must not only be tactful, but also understand how to effectively influence others. Everyone has a preference on how they need to be influenced and you should take the time to know each key individual's influencing preference.

Coach's Challenge

Since influencing is a critical component of advocacy, we recommend that you learn more about influencing tactics using our Influencing: The SID Way Workbook. This workbook is available on our website.

On the next two pages, circle the score you gave yourself for this statement in the Know Your Heading exercise on page 71 for this statement. Then, read the Coaches' Recommendations for your score.

Advocate: One who defends, vindicates, or espouses any cause by argument; a pleader; as, an advocate of free trade, an advocate of truth.

I advocate for customers within my organization.

Your Score: 1 (strongly disagree) 2 (disagree) 3 (agree) 4 (strongly agree)

Score: 1	Coaches' Recommendations

You scored low for this important item and we recommend that you include the steps to improve in this area as part of your development plan.

It is your responsibility to weigh the decisions and changes that occur in your organization and assess the impact they have on customers, particularly those that are your responsibility. If a decision or change will have a negative effect, it is customer advocacy to bring it to the attention of the appropriate people.

Identify what behaviors you will change to be a customer advocate and include them in your personal development plan.

Score: 2	Coaches' Recommendations

Being a customer advocate in your organization does not mean that you work hard for every position that the customer holds, even at the expense of your organization. Rather, it is developing a mindset that thinks of the customer first when making changes or decisions. Take the time to think about the effect that your organization's decisions or changes have on customers.

You recognize that you could improve in this area. List three steps you will take to demonstrate more customer advocacy within your organization:

1.

2.

3.

I advocate for customers within my organization.

Your Score: 1 (strongly disagree) 2 (disagree) 3 (agree) 4 (strongly agree)

Score: 3	Coaches' Recommendations

Leaders in the best organizations are strong advocates for their customers. As a leader you need to model this behavior in your organization. It is important that you continue to do this and make customer advocacy a part of your organization's culture.

Think about what more you could do to be a customer advocate in your organization. What behaviors could you change in this area?

Read Galbraith, <u>Designing the Customer-Centric Organization: A Guide to Strategy, Structure and Process</u> for ideas on making customer advocacy a part of your organization's culture.

Score: 4	Coaches' Recommendations

Leaders in the best organizations are strong advocates for their customers. Congratulations for modeling this behavior in your organization. It is important that you continue to do this and make customer advocacy a part of your organization's culture.

Ensure that people know that customer advocacy is not done at the expense of your organization. Rather, it is an awareness that decisions and changes in your organization have an effect on customers. This effect needs to be considered.

Read Galbraith, <u>Designing the Customer-Centric Organization: A Guide to Strategy, Structure and Process</u> for ideas on making customer advocacy a part of your organization's culture.

I advocate for customers within my organization.

List the development steps will you take to improve in this item.

1.

2.

3.

4.

Other Notes:

I strive to provide value to customers.

Your Coaches' Comments About This Item

Customers need to perceive that they are receiving value from you, whether consumers or businesses. Value means that they are getting more than they anticipated or they are paying less than anticipated. Value means a lot to customers and companies that provide "added value" are more likely to gain repeat business.

Providing value doesn't mean that you shortchange yourself or your business. Most value added products or services are little or no cost. But, the return of the investment can be substantial. You are not only providing more than expected; you are also taking great strides in improving your relationship with your customer.

Coach's Challenge

Think about when you have bought something or received a service and you perceived that you were receiving value. How did it make you feel? Did you return to that supplier or store or restaurant?

On the next two pages, circle the score you gave yourself for this statement in the Know Your Heading exercise on page 71 for this statement. Then, read the Coaches' Recommendations for your score.

"Price is what you pay. Value is what you get."
- Warren Buffett

"The well-satisfied customer will bring the repeat sale that counts."
- James Cash Penney

I strive to provide value to customers.

Your Score: 1 (strongly disagree) 2 (disagree) 3 (agree) 4 (strongly agree)

Score: 1	Coaches' Recommendations

Is there a particular reason that you do not strive to provide value to customers? List reasons you may have and determine how you can change the situation.

Perhaps you do not add value to customers because the culture of your organization does not promote it. In that case, find a leader you respect and discuss your misgivings about the culture and brainstorm ways to change it.

List the obstacles you face in striving to provide value to customers. Next to each obstacle describe how to overcome it to provide more value to customers.

Read Heil: One Size Fits All: Building Customer Relationships One Customer and One Employee at a Time.

Score: 2	Coaches' Recommendations

There is room for improvement in this important area. Think about why you do not strive to provide value to customers. What are the obstacles you face in doing so? Think about situations where you are the customer. You want to feel that you received the best value for your money. It is the same for your customers.

If customers do not feel you provide value to them they will not return as a customer; in addition to telling other potential customers that they should look elsewhere.

Providing customer value must be a priority for every successful organization. Think about three ways that you can contribute additional value to what you do for customers.

I strive to provide value to customers.

Your Score: 1 (strongly disagree) 2 (disagree) 3 (agree) 4 (strongly agree)

Score: 3	Coaches' Recommendations

This is a good score for this item but it is important enough for you to give some attention to improving to an even higher level. Understand that providing value is not necessarily something that has a negative impact on your organization. In fact, if your organization gains a reputation for providing the best value to customers it will be a tremendous asset when seeking new customers.

Score: 4	Coaches' Recommendations

This is an excellent score for this foundational item. Providing value to customers is often the most important behavior when building a relationship with a customer.

It should always be a part of an organization's culture to bring the best value to a customer. Use the organizational assessment Takeaway Tool in appendix B to evaluate your organization's customer focus. We recommend that you complete this assessment as part of your leadership team and have frank discussions about areas to improve, particularly if you and your colleagues do not feel you provide value to customers.

As a leader, take a proactive role in advocating customer value in the organization, including to internal customers.

I strive to provide value to customers.

List the development steps will you take to improve in this item.

1.

2.

3.

4.

Other Notes:

I am proactive in identifying customer needs and issues.

Your Coaches' Comments About This Item

Your customers have needs and issues that they deal with. If you can identify those needs you may very well be able to address them and build your business. Even if you cannot meet their needs in a specific area, you may be able to point them in the right direction. They will remember this and when they have a need that you can fulfill, you will be strongly considered.

It takes time to know and understand a customer's needs. They may not tell you specifically. Take the time to question your customers to learn as much as possible about their business and the problems they face. Learning more gives you the insight to truly partner with them to achieve success for both parties.

Coach's Challenge

Customer needs lie on two levels – organizational and individual. Consider your own situation. What are your organizational needs? What are your individual needs? Who can help you meet these needs?

On the next two pages, circle the score you gave yourself for this statement in the Know Your Heading exercise on page 71 for this statement. Then, read the Coaches' Recommendations for your score.

"Even if someone is already in your market space, ask yourself whether you can approach it from a different angle and thereby secure your own customer base."
- Benjamin Cohen

I am proactive in identifying customer needs and issues.

Your Score: 1 (strongly disagree) 2 (disagree) 3 (agree) 4 (strongly agree)

Score: 1	Coaches' Recommendations

Why do you consider yourself weak in this area? It is important in building a relationship with a customer to know their needs and understand the issues they deal with to be successful.

Knowing the customer's needs helps you understand your role in meeting the needs and helping them deal with their issues.

If you can help them meet their needs and resolve their problems they will be your customer for a long time.

List the obstacles you face in identifying customer's needs and issues. Why are these obstacles and what can you do about each?

Score: 2	Coaches' Recommendations

Why do you consider that you need improvement in this area? It is important in building a relationship with a customer to know their needs and understand the issues they deal with to be successful.

Knowing the customer's needs helps you understand your role in meeting the needs and helping them deal with their issues. This is the key to repeat business and a strong relationship with a customer

If you can help them meet their needs and resolve their problems they will be your customer for a long time.

For each customer, list their needs and issues that they face in their business. Be as detailed as possible in building the list.

I am proactive in identifying customer needs and issues.

Your Score: 1 (strongly disagree)   2 (disagree)   3 (agree)   4 (strongly agree)

Score: 3	Coaches' Recommendations

Good score for this item. However, there is always room for improvement. You may understand the importance of understanding a customer's needs, but how can you learn more about the issues they face that are impeding their success?

Strive to become a strategic partner with your customer by being as intimately involved with them as they will allow. If they respect your desire to understand and help them, they will call on you to help deal with their issues. Then, when they have a need that you can fulfill, you will be the first to be called upon.

We recommend building a form that identifies the needs for each customer. Maintain this list and share it with your colleagues. They may have information to add to it.

Score: 4	Coaches' Recommendations

This is an excellent score and we recommend that you continue to be proactive in identifying your customers' needs and issues.

What can you do to instill a similar mindset in your colleagues and across your organization? We have found the best way to do this is to continue to ask the questions, What are our customers' needs? What are the issues that our customers are dealing with on a daily basis? Then, it is easier to figure out how to meet the needs and help them deal with the issues they face.

A culture based on this is built by constantly keeping the customers' needs and issues at the forefront in any discussion related to them.

I am proactive in identifying customer needs and issues.

List the development steps will you take to improve in this item.

1.

2.

3.

4.

Other Notes:

I model customer-focused behaviors.

Your Coaches' Comments About This Item

As we grow older we are more selective in whose behaviors we model. Teenagers may model the behaviors of some very strange people. But, as we begin our professional life we choose others to model; hopefully people who are excellent leaders and successful. As you become more successful as a leader, more people will recognize your success and model your behaviors in hopes that it will lead to their success.

Your organization has a culture concerning how customers are treated and that culture is the summation of all the behaviors that are displayed. The first step in creating a customer-focus culture is for the leaders to demonstrate behaviors that are customer focused. Your staff will follow your lead; be careful in choosing the path you want them to take.

Coach's Challenge

What is your responsibility if you observe another leader in your organization displaying poor customer-focused behaviors?

On the next two pages, circle the score you gave yourself for this statement in the Know Your Heading exercise on page 71 for this statement. Then, read the Coaches' Recommendations for your score.

"Behavior is the mirror in which everyone shows their image."
- Johann Wolfgang von Goethe

I model customer-focused behaviors.

Your Score: 1 (strongly disagree) 2 (disagree) 3 (agree) 4 (strongly agree)

Score: 1	Coaches' Recommendations

Review the content presented earlier in this workbook regarding effective and ineffective customer-focused behaviors.

As a leader, you have the responsibility to model customer-focused behaviors so others adopt them.

Two assignments: First, complete the individual customer-focus assessment Takeaway Tool, in Appendix A.

Second, list three customer-focused behaviors that you will strengthen over the next 30 days. Write them on a 3x5 card and keep them where you can see them periodically throughout the day.

Score: 2	Coaches' Recommendations

Please review the content presented earlier in this workbook regarding effective and ineffective customer-focused behaviors.

As a leader, you have the responsibility to model customer-focused behaviors so others adopt them.

We recommend that you complete the customer focus individual assessment Takeaway Tool located in Appendix A. Use this tool for each customer and based on what you learn, identify any behaviors you think you should change.

I model customer-focused behaviors.

Your Score: 1 (strongly disagree) 2 (disagree) 3 (agree) 4 (strongly agree)

Score: 3	Coaches' Recommendations

This is a good score, but there is always room for improvement. It is critical that leaders model effective customer-focused behaviors. Everyone in an organization looks to their leaders to model behaviors. Keep this in mind and be conscious of the behaviors you are exhibiting in this area.

We recommend that you complete the customer focus individual assessment Takeaway Tool located in Appendix A. Use this tool for each customer and based on what you learn, identify any behaviors you think you should change.

Score: 4	Coaches' Recommendations

Because you scored well for this important item, your focus should be on your colleagues and other leaders in the organization. If a colleague or other leader does not model excellent customer-focused behaviors, it is incumbent upon you to bring it to their attention and help them to correct their behavior.

We recommend that you complete the Organization Customer-Focus assessment Takeaway Tool in Appendix B. We recommend using this tool with colleagues to assess the state of customer focus in your organization's culture.

Read Fogli: <u>Customer Service Delivery: Research and Best Practices</u>.

I model customer-focused behaviors.

List the development steps will you take to improve in this item.

1.

2.

3.

4.

Other Notes:

I proactively seek feedback from customers and listen to their comments.

Your Coaches' Comments About This Item

We encounter a lot of people who say that they value and welcome feedback. But, when they receive it they become crushed. Sometimes, this is because the person providing the feedback doesn't know how to give it; but more often it is because the person receiving it is not prepared for what they hear.

We also hear from companies that have excellent mechanisms to hear feedback from customers. They will tell you that many of their best ideas came from customers. Customers have a unique perspective of you and your business. Often, they can tell you what is not working well (and what is working well).

As a leader, you should value feedback as a gift. Either the gift will praise you and affirm that you are doing things right; or, it will tell you what you need to do better.

Coach's Challenge

If you were a customer, what feedback would you give about your company or organization? Think long and hard about this and role play a session where you are providing the feedback.

On the next two pages, circle the score you gave yourself for this statement in the Know Your Heading exercise on page 72 for this statement. Then, read the Coaches' Recommendations for your score.

"Feedback is the breakfast of champions."
- Ken Blanchard

I proactively seek feedback from customers and listen to their comments.

Your Score: 1 (strongly disagree) 2 (disagree) 3 (agree) 4 (strongly agree)

Score: 1	Coaches' Recommendations

Nothing is more valuable than feedback from your customers. You should always be seeking feedback both formally and informally.

Because you scored yourself low in this item, we recommend that you take steps immediately to change your behavior in this area. Do the following steps:

1. Think of each customer. What do you want to learn from them about your performance? List questions you want to ask that would give you good information.
2. Schedule time to visit or call the main contact with each customer. Listen to each customer's feedback.
3. For any constructive comments, determine a course of action to improve and communicate to the customer that brought up the item.

Score: 2	Coaches' Recommendations

Nothing is more valuable than feedback from your customers. You should always be seeking feedback both formally and informally.

Because you think your performance can improve in this item, we recommend that you take steps immediately to change your behavior.

Set a time to meet with or call each customer and ask their feedback on your organization's performance. Listen to their comments without responding. For any constructive comments, determine a course of action and tell the appropriate customer(s) of the actions you are taking to improve.

I proactively seek feedback from customers and listen to their comments.

Your Score: 1 (strongly disagree) 2 (disagree) 3 (agree) 4 (strongly agree)

Score: 3	Coaches' Recommendations

You recognize that you do well in this area but understand that you could do more to seek feedback from customers. Does your organization have a formal feedback process whereby someone contacts customers on a regular basis to gain feedback? This can be a written communication or call, but regardless of the method, it is effective.

If your organization receives feedback from customers, what happens? Consider having a system where feedback is communicated throughout the organization and ideas to improve are solicited. Those ideas can then be assigned to a responsible party for implementation. The actions taken should be communicated to the customer that provided the feedback.

Take steps to be more proactive in this area.

Score: 4	Coaches' Recommendations

Congratulations for doing well in this area. Continue to model this behavior by being proactive with customers and listening to them.

Consider your organization as a whole. Do you have formal feedback processes in place to solicit input from customers? If not, consider taking the lead in developing a written feedback questionnaire, online survey, or structured interviews to get customer feedback.

Every customer contact should include the question, "How are we doing and what could we do better?" Instill this in your followers and throughout the organization. Create a culture that values and acts upon customer feedback.

I proactively seek feedback from customers and listen to their comments.

List the development steps will you take to improve in this item.

1.

2.

3.

4.

Other Notes:

I proactively respond to customer requests.

Your Coaches' Comments About This Item

Customers constantly make requests and the customer-focused organization responds to the requests as quickly as possible. Responding to the request, however, is only half the issue; it is how you respond that determines whether you are customer focused or not. If you respond grudgingly, the customer will perceive that you are difficult to work with. Therefore, if you respond pleasantly, as part of the "team," the customer will be happier and want to continue working with you.

It is just as important to learn enough about the customer to be able to foresee their requests and prepare for them. This is a difficult skill to develop but the best leaders learn how to do it. Anticipating a customer's request enables you to be prepared and fulfill the request in a very short time, pleasing the customer.

Coach's Challenge

Think about how often you have made a request in a restaurant. Good servers may often anticipate your request and bring the "ketchup" before you ask for it. Others, less skilled, wait until you ask and then bring it to you with an attitude. Think about your attitude when responding to a customer request. Are you happy about it? What attitude do you show to the customer? Have you ever been able to anticipate a customer's request?

On the next two pages, circle the score you gave yourself for this statement in the Know Your Heading exercise on page 72 for this statement. Then, read the Coaches' Recommendations for your score.

"A business absolutely devoted to service will have only one worry about profits. They will be embarrassingly large."

\- Henry Ford

I proactively respond to customer requests.

Your Score: 1 (strongly disagree) 2 (disagree) 3 (agree) 4 (strongly agree)

Score: 1	Coaches' Recommendations

Customer requests are paramount and should take a priority over most things that you are doing. Since you scored yourself low in this item, it is important to understand why you did so. Do you not consider customer requests important? If that is the case, consider who is "paying the bills." Are you too busy with other priorities? If so, talk to someone who can help you prioritize your work better so you have the flexibility to respond to customer requests.

Do you think it is someone else's responsibility to respond to a customer's request? If so, take ownership until it is determined who should be responsible.

There are many excuses for not being responsive to customer requests. None of them are good.

Score: 2	Coaches' Recommendations

You feel you could improve in this area and we congratulate you on recognizing this. Responding to customer requests is critical in any business. You may consider the request to be unreasonable, but if so you still have an obligation to respond in a tactful manner.

Valid requests should become your top priority. If you feel overwhelmed and unable to respond in a timely manner, get help. There is a saying that "every customer wants to feel like they are your only customer." This is very important to remember and think about when you are prioritizing your efforts. Small customers can become big customers if the relationship is nurtured and they feel that you treat them equal to a much larger customer. This treatment is often based on how quickly and thoroughly you respond to customers.

I proactively respond to customer requests.

Your Score: 1 (strongly disagree) 2 (disagree) 3 (agree) 4 (strongly agree)

Score: 3	Coaches' Recommendations

You are proactive in responding to customer requests and we recommend that you continue to model this behavior.

Think about ways that you can be even more proactive by anticipating customer requests and providing your response before being asked. As you learn more about each customer and their needs, you will become more adept at being able to anticipate customer requests.

Continue to improve in this area and work with your team and colleagues to be proactive.

Score: 4	Coaches' Recommendations

Since you excel in this important area, it is appropriate that you model this behavior across your organization. Work toward creating a culture that is known for responsiveness to customers.

One method to help create this culture is to reward team members who are proactive in responding to customers. Simply identifying this behavior in a meeting and showing recognition will help it become part of your culture.

I proactively respond to customer requests.

List the development steps will you take to improve in this item.

1.

2.

3.

4.

Other Notes:

I seek to understand my customer's key issues.

Your Coaches' Comments About This Item

Your organization has issues. Think about it – you must meet payroll, you must do well in the marketplace, you must deal with unexpected problems in your operation. Everyday you are faced with issues.

Customers are in the same situation. They have issues that affect their business. But, what does this have to do with you? Our studies have shown that companies that understand their customer's key issues and work toward helping them resolve the issues get more business. You begin to become more of a strategic partner with your customers because they know you care about what is an obstacle to their success and want to work with them to overcome the obstacle.

Coach's Challenge

Think about your organization. What are your key issues? How would you feel if another organization worked with you to resolve the key issues? Think about yourself. What key issues do you face?

On the next two pages, circle the score you gave yourself for this statement in the Know Your Heading exercise on page 72 for this statement. Then, read the Coaches' Recommendations for your score.

"Our business is about technology, yes. But it's also about operations and customer relationships."

- Michael Dell

I seek to understand my customer's key issues.

Your Score: 1 (strongly disagree)   2 (disagree)   3 (agree) 4 (strongly agree)

Score: 1	Coaches' Recommendations

Understanding your customer's business and how they fit into their marketplace is important information to know. Why did you score low for this item? Perhaps you feel you do not have the time. Or, perhaps you feel this information is not important.

On the contrary, the small amount of time you take to understand your customer and their business is a good investment. It will help you understand their issues and lead to your identifying ways to help them succeed.

List each customer and describe what you know about them and their business. Then, list the issues each customer faces in their marketplace. Keep this information updated regularly and seek out information that is missing.

Score: 2	Coaches' Recommendations

It is important to learn as much as possible about your customers. Not only does it help in building a relationship but it also gives you more insight into what their needs may be.

We recommend that you set aside time every few days to research your customers. Go beyond just looking at their web site. Ask others what they have heard about your customers. Follow the trends in their industry. Ask yourself, "What problems and issues do they face?"

As an exercise, list each customer, write down what you know about them, and then identify the issues that they face in their marketplace. Push yourself to be as detailed as possible. You may find you know more about some customers than others. If so, focus your research on those with the least information.

I seek to understand my customer's key issues.

Your Score: 1 (strongly disagree) 2 (disagree) 3 (agree) 4 (strongly agree)

Score: 3	Coaches' Recommendations

Continue to seek to learn as much as possible about your customers' business and the issues that they face. Think about how you can get better at this.

Consider how you can disseminate the appropriate information to others in your organization. Perhaps shared files, if you have the capability, will work. Or, take time during a regularly scheduled meeting to briefly discuss information learned about important customers.

Regularly check each customer's website, as well as their competitors' websites.

Stress to others in your organization that it is important to know each customer's key issues so you can strategize how to help them in their marketplace.

Score: 4	Coaches' Recommendations

This is a very good score for this item. Continue to seek to learn as much as possible about your customers' business and the issues that they face.

Consider how you can disseminate the appropriate information to others in your organization. Perhaps shared files, if you have the capability, will work. Or, take time during a regularly scheduled meeting to briefly discuss information learned about important customers.

Regularly check each customer's website, as well as their competitors' websites.

Stress to others in your organization that it is important to know each customer's key issues so you can strategize how to help them in their marketplace.

I seek to understand my customer's key issues.

List the development steps will you take to improve in this item.

1.

2.

3.

4.

Other Notes:

I am "easy to do business with."

Your Coaches' Comments About This Item

Why make work more difficult than it already is? Don't you like to work with certain people or organizations just because they are enjoyable to work with? Why not strive to ensure that customers want to work with you?

Some people in an organization strive to create a "we-them" environment with customers. This never works well for customer focus. When this behavior is modeled to others on your team in inevitably creates conflict with customers. Strive, instead, to create a team environment with your customers.

Coach's Challenge

What does it mean to be "easy to work with?" What personality traits lead to this perception?

Do you think your customers are easy to work with? If not, what can you do to create a better working environment?

On the next two pages, circle the score you gave yourself for this statement in the Know Your Heading exercise on page 72 for this statement. Then, read the Coaches' Recommendations for your score.

"Always be yourself, express yourself, have faith in yourself, do not go out and look for a successful personality and duplicate it."
- Bruce Lee

I am "easy to do business with."

Your Score: 1 (strongly disagree) 2 (disagree) 3 (agree) 4 (strongly agree)

Score: 1	**Coaches' Recommendations**

No one likes to work with someone who is difficult and not cooperative. We recommend that you immediately change whatever behaviors are keeping you from being easy to work with. Take time to review your behaviors and identify what you can and should change.

This does not mean that you do not look out for the interests of your organization. On the contrary, being easy to work with helps your organization in the long run. As someone once said, "If I want to work with you I will find a way to give you work; if I don't want to work with you, I will not give you (and your organization) any work."

Include steps to improve in this area in your development plan. It is critical that you focus on changing.

Score: 2	**Coaches' Recommendations**

You have identified that you need improvement in this area. Think about what behaviors would make you easier to work with. Do you drive a hard bargain with customers to the advantage of your organization? Do you avoid socializing and getting to know the customer better?

List three behaviors you could change that would make you easier to work with. Over the next month, focus on changing these behaviors. Then, continue by identifying additional behaviors that you could change and focus on improving them.

Customers choose who they work with and if you are not easy to work with you may find you and your organization without customers.

I am "easy to do business with."

Your Score: 1 (strongly disagree) 2 (disagree) 3 (agree) 4 (strongly agree)

Score: 3	Coaches' Recommendations

Good score for this item; however, we challenge you to ask your customers if they agree with you. Most likely they will but it is interesting to know whether there is a "disconnect" between what you think and what customers think. It doesn't hurt to simply ask customers, "Am I (or we) easy to work with? What could I (we) do better to make this relationship work to help make your organization a success."

Continue to model the behaviors that make you easy to work with. Others will adopt these behaviors when they see that you are successful in working with customers.

Score: 4	Coaches' Recommendations

What attributes make you easy to work with? Identifying those attributes can help you mentor others in your organization that may be less than easy to get along with.

Customers desire to work with someone who is cheerful, optimistic and helpful. They also want someone who will problem solve and put their interests as a priority.

Use the Organizational Customer-Focus Assessment in Appendix B to help assess how easy you and your colleagues are to work with. Take steps to create a culture that makes customers "want to choose you."

I am "easy to do business with."

List the development steps will you take to improve in this item.

1.

2.

3.

4.

Other Notes:

I follow through with what I commit to a customer.

Your Coaches' Comments About This Item

You have probably heard that relationships are built on commitment. If you want a relationship with your customers, base it on keeping your commitments. Commitments are like trust – if you keep them you have a customer for life; but, the first time you do not fulfill a commitment you will lose a customer.

It may see unfair sometimes – not being able to "take a pass" sometimes and forget about a commitment that may require extra work or effort. But, you must always remember, your competitors are knocking at your customer's door everyday just waiting for you to slip up. Don't give them the opportunity to walk in the door – keep all your commitments.

Coach's Challenge

Has anyone made a commitment to you and not delivered? What did you think about them? Did it damage your relationship with them?

On the next two pages, circle the score you gave yourself for this statement in the Know Your Heading exercise on page 72 for this statement. Then, read the Coaches' Recommendations for your score.

"A relationship requires a lot of work and commitment."
- Greta Scacchi

I follow through with what I commit to a customer.

Your Score: 1 (strongly disagree) 2 (disagree) 3 (agree) 4 (strongly agree)

Score: 1	**Coaches' Recommendations**

We appreciate your honesty in assessing your behaviors in this area. We hope you realize that making changes in this area is critical to your success. If you consistently fail to meet commitments you make to customers your performance will come into question.

Record all commitments you make in a small notebook. Include when the commitment is due and what obstacles may keep you from achieving it. If you see that you cannot achieve a commitment you have made to a customer, be proactive and tell the customer. They will appreciate your honesty much more than your being late or forgetting about the commitment.

Work hard in this area. Your performance and reputation are at stake.

Score: 2	**Coaches' Recommendations**

You feel that you can and should improve in this area. What obstacles do you face in following through on commitments? Clear out the obstacles and you will be able to follow through 100% of the time.

Be careful, however, that you do not over commit. Be realistic in promises that you make and do not promise something when you cannot deliver.

One technique that may be helpful is to have a small notebook to record all commitments you make to a customer. Keep the notebook with you at all times and review it throughout the day. Hopefully, this technique will prevent you from forgetting the commitments you have made.

I follow through with what I commit to a customer.

Your Score: 1 (strongly disagree) 2 (disagree) 3 (agree) 4 (strongly agree)

Score: 3	Coaches' Recommendations

Good score for this item, but you clearly think you could do better. Try taking the attitude that you will not only follow through on commitments you have made to a customer, but you will exceed the commitment. If you tell a customer you will deliver something within two days, deliver it in one day. Always think about how you can add value to what you are delivering.

What obstacles do you face in following through on commitments? Clear out the obstacles and you will be able to follow through 100% of the time.

Be careful, however, that you do not over commit. Be realistic in promises that you make and do not promise when you cannot deliver.

Score: 4	Coaches' Recommendations

Excellent! Now, does this follow through to others in your organization? Does your organization have a reputation for always following through on commitments? If not, you must take steps to change the culture to one that is noted for always following through.

Your goal is to not only fulfill your customers' expectations but to exceed them. Customer focus is all about delighting the customer. Often, following through on even the most mundane commitments builds your reputation as someone that is attentive to the needs of the customer.

Continue to model this behavior and to remind others when they make commitments that they must follow through 100% of the time.

I follow through with what I commit to a customer.

List the development steps will you take to improve in this item.

1.

2.

3.

4.

Other Notes:

"The learning and knowledge that we have, is, at the most, but little compared with that of which we are ignorant."

- Plato

Your Development Plan

If you recall our discussion of the SID™ Model, having a development plan is critical to improving your behaviors and skills. The development plan guides your actions as you strive to improve and helps you stay focused.

In this section, you will create your Customer-Focus development plan. The plan should be based on your scores in the Know Your Heading self assessment and the information provided in the Coaches' Itinerary and Coaches' Recommendations for each item.

Use the following steps to create your development plan:

1. Review your scores for each item in the Know Your Heading self assessment (pages 71 and 72). Select your lowest scored items.
2. Review your coaches' development recommendations for each item.
3. Review the general recommendations for customer focus in the Coaches' Guidance section.
4. Review the appendices and Coaches' Bookshelf for further tools and resources.
5. Using the template provided in this section, complete the development plan for each selected item. Follow these steps:
    a. In the left column, list the specific actions you will take. The statement in this column should always begin with a verb since it is an action that will take place. Be as descriptive as possible in this column.
    b. In the next column, identify any resources you will need to accomplish the action.
    c. The next column should indicate a date that you will review your progress in taking the action. This will tell you whether you are on track to achieve your completion date.
    d. Your projected completion date should be indicated in the next column.
6. After you have made progress in improving your skills and behaviors in the selected items, create another development plan to continue improvement. At this point you may want to consider selecting some of you strongest items and develop a plan to emphasize those strengths in your position. Or, your focus may move to organizational development to raise the bar of customer-focused skills and behaviors across the organization. Regardless, continue to create and use the development plan.

In the left column, list the specific steps you will take. Be as descriptive as possible. The next column is used to identify resources you may need to help improve. The following column sets a date for you to "check progress" toward completing the action. The right column specifies the date when you will be completed.

Here's an example of one action:

ACTION	NEEDED RESOURCES	PROGRESS CHECK DATE	COMPLETION DATE
List the ways that I can add value to customers.	Time – about 1 hour to think about it. Take notes in a notebook for future reference. Help – Brainstorm ideas with James and Kelly who do a good job in this area and know me well enough to give me feedback.	2/17	3/30

MY DEVELOPMENT PLAN FOR CUSTOMER FOCUS

ACTIONS	NEEDED RESOURCES	PROGRESS CHECK DATE	COMPLETION DATE

ACTIONS	NEEDED RESOURCES	PROGRESS CHECK DATE	COMPLETION DATE

ACTIONS	NEEDED RESOURCES	PROGRESS CHECK DATE	COMPLETION DATE

ACTIONS	NEEDED RESOURCES	PROGRESS CHECK DATE	COMPLETION DATE

Appendices

Appendix A – Takeaway Tool 1

Takeaway Tools are designed to help you improve your skills, behaviors and results for this competency.

Customer Focus Worksheet/Checklist

This tool provides you guidance on gaining information about customers and directs you through a sequence of steps to identify how you can improve your customer focus with each internal and external customer.

TAKEAWAY TOOL 1 – CUSTOMER FOCUS

CUSTOMER FOCUS WORKSHEET/CHECKLIST

Identify your key customers and use the following checklist to determine how customer-focused you are with this customer. Duplicate this checklist to use for each of your key customers.

ITEM	CK	COMMENTS
I know this customer's key business strategies.		
I know this customer's products or services.		
I know this customer's key personnel, their roles and their responsibilities. I know who reports to whom.		
I have learned as much information as possible about each key person in the customer's organization including birthdays, previous positions, and hobbies.		
I know this customer's buying processes.		
I have introduced key people in my organization to key people in the customer's organization.		
I have learned this customer's key issues.		
I focus my conversations with this customer on his/her key issues and to learn about their business.		
I seek opportunities to add value to this customer.		

ITEM	CK	COMMENTS
I brief my team members on the customer's needs and issues before they interact with them.		
I have developed a strategy to delight this customer.		
I stay in reasonable contact with this customer.		
I work with the customer to solve problems.		
I listen to the customer and ask clarifying questions.		
I have identified the obstacles that this customer faces in their drive for success.		
I have identified the obstacles that my organization faces in dealing with this customer.		
I have initiated actions to overcome each obstacle that my organization faces in dealing with this customer.		
I know this customer's competitors.		
I regularly review this customer's website.		
I receive Google™ Alerts about this customer.		
I ensure that I communicate as much information as possible about a customer to the appropriate people in my organization.		

Appendix B – Takeaway Tool 2

Takeaway Tools are designed to help you improve your skills, behaviors and results for this competency.

Organizational Customer Focus Assessment

This assessment enables you to gauge how well your organization demonstrates customer focus. You can perform this assessment individually or work as a team. We recommend that if you do this as a team exercise, that each participant completes the assessment individually and then discusses the responses as a group. For each item the team should develop action items to improve.

TAKEAWAY TOOL 2 – CUSTOMER FOCUS

ORGANIZATIONAL CUSTOMER FOCUS WORKSHEET

The following worksheet can be used to assess your organization's level of customer focus. Each leader should complete the worksheet individually and then have a group discussion comparing results. The outcome should be an action plan to improve your customer-focus culture.

ITEM	CK	COACHES' REMARKS AND YOUR ACTIONS TO IMPROVE
We know our customers and can rank them in order of importance to our business.		Each leader should list customers and rank them in order of importance. In the group discussion the lists can be compared.
When we visit customers we are dressed appropriately and perform professionally.		Every customer interaction should be as professional as possible.
All of our customer touchpoints make a strong positive impression.		Be sure to consider touchpoints such as your reception area and personnel, attendance at tradeshows and industry meetings.

ITEM	CK	COACHES' REMARKS AND YOUR ACTIONS TO IMPROVE
Our presentations are based on the customer's needs and learning about their key issues.		Presentations should be about the customer, not you.
We maintain a database of information about each customer.		This database should be regularly maintained and contain information about customers and every interaction with the customer (at every level).
We communicate regularly with each customer through phone calls and e-mails.		The results of these calls should be noted in the customer database.
We regularly communicate with all customers through a newsletter or blog. In this communication we provide information valuable to all customers and highlight key changes in our organization.		Take every opportunity to communicate with customers.

ITEM	CK	COACHES' REMARKS AND YOUR ACTIONS TO IMPROVE
We regularly ask ourselves what we could do better to improve our customer focus.		Develop a schedule to regularly evaluate and take improvement steps in customer focus.
We regularly review every customer's website and publications to learn the latest information about the company, its products or services, and personnel.		If something is learned about a customer, ensure that you have a method in place for the information to be shared with all your key people who interact with a customer.
We use Google™ Alert to learn the latest news about each customer.		Google alert will notify you of any published information about a company or individual through e-mail on a daily basis.
We are aware of important dates for key customers, such as birthdays and awards, and we acknowledge these events.		Be aware of each customer's gift receiving policies and be careful not to violate.

ITEM	CK	COACHES' REMARKS AND YOUR ACTIONS TO IMPROVE
We seek out opportunities to write articles and give presentations with customer personnel		Collaborating with a customer to write articles or deliver presentations builds your relationship with them.
We regularly seek feedback from our customers through interviews and survey instruments.		Be sure to act on feedback and notify customers of the actions you take.
We have a social media strategy that enables us to engage our customers, provide valuable information, and channels for customers to contact us.		A social media strategy is essential for any business in today's world.
Our organization's website is professional looking and provides opportunities for customers to interact with us and gain valuable information.		Make a visit to your website a valuable experience for any customer who visits.

Appendix C – Coaches' Bookshelf

Fogli, L. <u>Customer Service Delivery: Research and Best Practices</u>. San Francisco: Jossey-Bass. 2005.

> *This book taps into business, marketing, and psychological research to provide a wealth of knowledge about customer service. Includes contributions from some of the world's best known experts in customer service. It provides a framework for customer service as a process and an outcome. This book is strongly recommended for those in service organizations.*

Galbraith, J. <u>Designing the Customer-Centric Organization: A Guide to Strategy, Structure, and Process</u>. San Francisco: Jossey-Bass. 2005.

> *Provides leaders with a comprehensive customer-centric organizational model that clearly shows how to put in place an infrastructure that is organized around the demands of the customer.*

Heil, Gary; Parker, Tom; and Stephens, Deborah. <u>One Size Fits One: Building Customer Relationships One Customer and One Employee at a Time</u>. 1999. Wiley.

> *Provides the ten rules for what customers want – in their own blunt words – and shows your company how to develop the personal relationships necessary to build loyalty. Another highlight is the presentation of an organizational structure to support greater customer/employee relationships and a better, stronger company.*

Miller, Ray. <u>That's Customer Focus!: The Overworked and Underappreciated Manager's Guide to Creating a Customer-Focused Organization</u>. BookSurge Publishing. 2008.

> *Provides detailed, step-by-step instructions on what to do to create customer focus throughout your entire organization. It provides 12 best practices and strategies and many examples, stories, and case studies. It also includes exercises and worksheets to help achieve greater customer focus in your organization, company, department or team.*

Appendix D – 4P's Leadership Competency Model™

We began our analysis of leadership competencies years ago and struggled to put a framework together that covered the necessary skills and behaviors to measure leadership abilities. Our work progressed as we designed and developed leadership assessments for university leaders from Deans to Vice Presidents to Presidents and others. At that point we began to refine our assessment of the major skills and behaviors necessary for successful and effective leadership and out of this research and work we formulated our 4P Leadership Competency Model™.

Although there are hundreds of leadership books and models of competencies, we felt a wide competency-based approach was best to fit our Self-Initiated Development Model. On the next page we list these 30 leadership competencies. A workbook similar to this one is being developed for each. You can order workbooks as they are completed at www.thesidway.com.

In addition, you can complete a master self assessment that covers all 30 competencies at our website. This can be used to determine which of the competencies are strengths and which you should focus on first for improvement.

As your coaches, we wish you the best and hope that you will use this workbook and the others to become a better leader. You can also visit our leadership blog at the www.thesidway.com website to keep up to date on the progress of our workbooks and learn more about leadership and management topics.

BenchMark Learning International's

4P's Competency Model™

Persuasive Vision

Creativity
Influencing
Inspiration
Motivation
Planning
Strategic Thinking

People Skills

Change Leadership
Commitment to Diversity
Communications
Conflict Management
Interpersonal Skills
Negotiation
Problem Solving
Talent Management
Teamwork

Positive Results

Business Development
Commitment to Quality
Customer Focus
Decision Making
Financial Management
Focus on Results
Technical Skills
Time Management

Personal Character

Courage
Credibility
Followership
Initiative
Integrity
Stress Management
Trust

Appendix E – Using the SID™ Model for Organizational Improvement

After completing this workbook for Customer Focus, you can see how it helps you individually improve your skills and behaviors. However, we feel that it is important that organizations use this information to change their culture to be more customer focused. Individual improvement is a priority, but it is when an organization embraces customer focus that it becomes most impactful in the organization's culture and in the marketplace.

The following are some ideas to help your organization improve in customer focus.

- Recommend that all leaders and managers in the organization use this workbook and the SID™ Model to improve their individual customer-focused behaviors. If leaders and managers model excellent behaviors, others will follow the lead.

- Evaluate your organization's customer focus by talking with customers. You could also develop a survey or conduct interviews to gain information from customers about how well your organization does in this area. Routinely evaluate your customer-focused behaviors by talking with customers at least quarterly.

- Establish a measurement system to identify your customer focus and delight levels against your stated customer focus goals. Everyone in the organization needs to know what the goal is, how it is measured, and how to reach the stated goals.

- Reward those individuals who exemplify excellent customer focus. This can be done inexpensively with an award, such as a plaque or by giving some other tangible benefit such as a gift certificate. Be sure to communicate this action and the behavior that earned it across the organization.

- If you learn from observation, self assessments, or customers that customer focus is a weak area across the organization, assign a leader to initiate a training program or education event to address good customer-focused behaviors. Use the SID™ Model to help individuals develop their skills and behaviors and to drive a customer-focused culture.

- Ask your staff for their ideas on how to improve customer focus. Getting everyone involved helps create a culture that is more impactful in this area. Consider creating a "customer-focused team" that monitors customer focus and initiates programs to improve.

About Your Coaches

Ben and Sidney McDonald are co-founders of BenchMark Learning International. Both are respected executive coaches and facilitators of leadership programs. Their primary work has been with Fortune 500 corporations and some of the country's leading universities including Dartmouth College, Johns Hopkins Medical University, Illinois Institute of Technology, and Case Western Reserve University.

Corporate clients have included Cisco Systems, CB&I, KBR, Skanska USA, Ericsson, Siemens and others. Both specialize in the design, development, and delivery of leadership programs. Both are also experienced leadership development consultants and work with organizations in improving their leadership and talent management systems.

They have held leadership positions in their professional career and have translated this experience into their leadership development programs and executive coaching. Until the founding of BenchMark Learning in 1999, Ben held leadership positions with GTE, McDonnell Douglas, and International Learning Systems. Prior to founding Benchmark Learning, Sidney was a leader at US West for over 17 years in sales, management, and training and development.

If you have any questions for your coaches on the content of this book, the SID™ process, or would like ideas to help you or your group exceed expectations in customer focus, you may contact us at questions@thesidway.com.